FROM FAITH TO FAITHFUL

FULLY EXPRESSING OUR FAITH THROUGH LOVE TO A WORLD THAT NEEDS TO SEE IT

ANDY BUCKWALTER

Copyright © 2019 Andy Buckwalter
All rights Reserved

Printed in the United States of America

Published by Author Academy Elite
P.O. Box 43, Powell, OH 43035
www.AuthorAcademyElite.com

All rights reserved. No part of this publication may be reproduced, stored in a retrieval system, or transmitted in any form or by any means—for example, electronic, photocopy, recording—without the prior written permission of the publisher. The only exception is brief quotations in printed reviews.

Paperback: 978-1-64085-623-3
Hardback: 978-1-64085-624-0
Library of Congress Control Number: 2019936335
Author Academy Elite, Powell, Ohio

Scripture quotations are taken from the Holy Bible, New Living Translation, copyright ©1996, 2004, 2007, 2013, 2015 by Tyndale House Foundation. Used by permission of Tyndale House Publishers, Inc., Carol Stream, Illinois 60188. All rights reserved.

Praise for *From Faith to Faithful*

If I could only use one word to describe this book it would be relatable. Andy brings abstract ideas about faith down to earth through funny quips and hilarious stories. You'll want to share this book with a friend.

—Zanetta Kok, Founder of Kitty Town Coffee

Andy Buckwalter's ***From Faith to Faithful*** is a refreshing look at faith in our day to day lives. Too many books on faith are scripture-laden, too serious, and stale. Not so with Andy Buckwalter's writing style. Andy's not afraid to talk about real issues, doesn't like to waste time, and likes to tell it like it is. Luckily his sense of humor lets him do this without getting preachy! If you or someone you care about wants to take the next step in your faith, grab a copy of ***From Faith to Faithful***.

—Mark LaMaster, Founder and CEO of
Uplifting Dads, LLC
Author of *The Dad Drift* and other
faith-based fatherhood books

Andy has the unique ability to make you snort with laughter while two sentences later challenging your preconceived notions of what it means to live faithfully. He uses real life experiences to break down barriers, then challenges us to stop pretending, to stop faking it, and instead be real.

—Justin Hendricks, Student Ministry Director,
LCBC York campus

What would faith look like if we weren't afraid to be real with our life? Andy takes you on a journey of real day-to-day faith issues with humor and life stories that keep you entertained but speak volumes. Learn how to live your faith each day by being honest with yourself and stepping out of your comfort zone.

—W. Paige Green, Father to three amazing boys

As a pastor, I appreciate how Andy highlights the fact that we're not called to be superficial Christians, but that we're all a work in progress. His writing is real, raw and he's not afraid to talk about the tough subjects. His vulnerability and sense of humor will draw you in as you read From Faith to Faithful!

—Richie Reeder, Pastor, Reclamation Church

If you are looking for a book that will introduce you to a believer's walk of faith to faithfulness; full of practical spiritual insight and wisdom; challenging; and delivered in a fun, even laugh out loud style that keeps you turning the pages, I guess this one is as good as any. I didn't really read the whole thing. But I know Andy and he's a good guy. I'm pretty sure he said some good stuff in here. Oh, and there aren't any pictures. So, there's that.

—Melody Box, Author of *He Can Be Trusted*
Founder of MelodyBoxInspires.com

To my girls

Nobody has inspired me to express my faith more than you.

Contents

Chapter 1	Business School Theology...............	1
Chapter 2	I Survived The Van Flatulence Of 2002 ...	9
Chapter 3	Weekly Forced Social Interaction	16
Chapter 4	Nobody Actually Likes Swimming	22
Chapter 5	The Time I Participated In A Mandatory Fitness Assessment	29
Chapter 6	We Can Do Better Than This..........	37
Chapter 7	A Clown In The Rain	44
Chapter 8	Barbequed Stuffed Animals...........	52
Chapter 9	Substitute Person....................	60
Chapter 10	Holy	65
Chapter 11	Laundry, Nail Care, Chinese Food	75

Chapter 12	The Easy Part	84
Chapter 13	My Little Girl	93
Chapter 14	Those Stupid People Are People	99
Chapter 15	Cheers	109
Chapter 16	Your One Thing	115
Chapter 17	Pete	124
Chapter 18	Homeless: *Adjective*	132
Chapter 19	We Can Do Better Than This. Part 2 . . .	140
Chapter 20	Keep Baby Asleep	148
Chapter 21	Handing Out Love From A Cardboard Box	158
Chapter 22	The Last Chapter	165

Notes 169
Thank You 173
Connect With Andy 175
About The Author 179

Business School Theology

My First Day Of Class

When I was twenty-five, I decided it was time for a change. So, I decided to go to grad-school to study business. (You know, like a man). I had a degree in youth ministry from Messiah College, but that really only qualified me for one job, and I didn't want it. So, I applied to one school, got in, and before long, it was time for my first class.

I got to class nice and early and took a seat. As others began trickling in, I overheard some of their conversations, one of which stood out to me. It turned out that two classes had been scheduled for this classroom, and we weren't sure which should stay and which should go. I was looking for Business 501. So, when I heard that one student from a business class was going to a different classroom, I went with him.

We arrived in the new classroom with minutes to spare. I had made an agreement with myself that I was going to sit in the front row in business school. I was usually a back row kind of guy, but I wanted to take myself out of my comfort zone in this small way. So, I took a seat in the front on the far side of the classroom; the professor finally arrived, and began taking attendance.

Now, my initials are A.B. So, when I wasn't one of the first people called, I found it strange, but since I had only signed up for the class that afternoon, I thought maybe I just wasn't on the list yet. I waited until the attendance was over, at which point the professor went straight into saying, "Okay, you're all here for Business 513..."

Rut Roe...I was in the wrong class.

Hot.

That's the first thing that I remember happening. Suddenly, I was really hot. It was January so I was wearing a sweater anyway, and I started sweating profusely. Now, I had a decision to make.

Should I just sit through this class? It is a business class...

But I'm missing part of the class I'm supposed to be in!

Yes, but everyone will know you're in the wrong class and that you're an idiot! Why did you sit in the front row!?

I don't know!!!

Eventually, I did the only thing I could do. I got up, grabbed my bag and my big awkward winter coat, slowly and noticeably shuffled all the way down the completely full front row, behind my new peers, avoided eye contact with the professor, and scuttled out of the classroom.

I then started tearing my bag apart. Which room was my class in? Was it the first classroom I went to? What number was it again? Is it neither? I'm now like 15 minutes late to a class I was already nervous about attending! I read the whole syllabus, and I still can't find the room number anywhere! I'm panicking, and everyone in the hallway can tell I'm panicking, no matter how nonchalantly I'm tearing through my bag as fast as I can.

Finally, I realize it says it right at the top of the page, clear as day:

Business 501
Rm 215
Tuesdays 6:15

Wait…Tuesday?

I wasn't in the wrong classroom. I was there on the wrong day.

Instantly, I felt relief, and mortification, in equal parts. I calmly put my bag back together, slowly walked back to my car, and went home. My first day of business school was done.

My Second Day Of Class

Needless to say, on the first day of my second semester, I showed up plenty early. I was in a new building I had never been to before, so I gave myself a lot of time. I was looking for room 218 in the ARC building, whatever that is. I found the building, went to the second floor and looked for the room.

Everything was going great. I'm walking down the hallway; I'm like fifteen minutes early, and the rooms are progressing appropriately. 212… 214…216…220… Wait. What? How did I walk right past it? Let's try again, 220…216…What? *This is why we show up early.*

So, I looked again, and it turns out I had missed a room. Right in-between rooms 216 and 220 was a bathroom. And overtop of this bathroom was a sign that read "218." So, I went in.

As you would expect it was just a room with stalls, sinks, toilets, and paper towel dispensers. I said out loud, "This seems unlikely."

I left the restroom and found someone who works in one of the offices who explains to me that there are two ARC buildings (Seriously?), and I am clearly in the wrong one. I felt less responsible this time, but I now had absolute proof that I have to show up early to class.

Round 3

In my third semester I arrived early again. This time, all was going well. I'm looking for room 240. So, I'm walking down the hall, and the rooms are progressing appropriately. I can tell by the length of the hall that I'm in one of the very last classrooms. 234… 236…238… brick wall.

Turns out…There is no room 240! It's not that I couldn't find it; I wasn't in the wrong building or there on the wrong day. *The room just didn't exist.* Eventually, the entire class had congregated in the hallway, and we just picked a new classroom. But again, you always show up early on the first day of class.

After this, when I arrived at class early, I started standing up before class started and asking what class everyone was there for just to make sure. And guess what...?

On the first day of my last semester, I stood up asked what class this was, and I got two answers. Somewhat poetically, just like my first semester, the school had scheduled two classes in one classroom.

This time, I didn't leave.

Feeling Outgunned

I hope these stories made you laugh. They are pretty funny looking back, but the truth is, there was a moment on my first night of "class" where I was sitting in a hallway, realizing that I had come to class on the wrong night. At that moment, I *really* didn't feel qualified to be in business school. I *definitely* didn't feel like I knew the answers. And I, *for sure*, didn't want to do it anymore. I really felt out of place.

When I started business school, I didn't know anything about business concepts. I had studied youth ministry in college, and believe it or not; we didn't discuss a lot of accounting, financing, or marketing strategies in my ministry classes. So, on the first night when I heard other students discussing 'accounts payable,' 'target markets,' and 'return on investments' I felt really outgunned, and I wasn't sure if I was going to be able to finish the program.

In business school there are rules, and the biggest one is—you don't pass the class if you don't understand the concepts. Pretty simple rule really, but it's a big one. You don't pass the class if you don't pass the test, and you don't get the diploma if you don't pass the classes.

You don't get to move on until you pass the class. You don't get to put "business degree" on your resume until you have your diploma. Not until you have mastered the concepts. *All* of the concepts—even the hard ones.

You can't go into a job interview and tell them that you were able to pass the first few classes, but once they started getting hard, you decided to quit. That would probably be worse than just not bringing it up at all. You can't say:

> I passed most of the classes, but there was this one part I'm just not sure about.

> There are a few parts that I still have questions about actually.

> I don't know all of the answers, but I can usually avoid those.

> I'm really not confident that I can do a job that requires me to use this information.

> I didn't feel like taking the last few classes.

That's not how it works. You don't get the title until you've mastered it all.

I think this is how some of us approach Christianity, and we shouldn't. I think a lot of us get caught up in the idea that we can't do anything until we've mastered all of the concepts. We feel like we don't get the title "Christian" until we've answered all of the questions and passed all of the tests. And that's just not the case. The truth is, you really only need to have one part figured out, that Jesus loves you, and you're in. That's all it takes.

We get to put "Christian" on our life's resume as soon as we decide to. Wherever we are, God is ready to use us there. We don't have to wait until we reach a certain level. We don't need to have all the answers. We don't have to wait until we possess some kind of qualification. We don't have to accomplish something first. We don't even need to have a good attitude all the time. Wherever we are, God is ready to use us. We're ready to put our faith into action.

The Only Thing That Matters

There are not going to be many Bible verses in this book, but I figured we should, at least, have a good one for the theme of this book. So, here it is. It is Galatians 5:6b, and it goes like this,

> *The only thing that counts is faith expressing itself through love.*

Yes, we need more context. Yes I'm quoting it outside of that context, and yes, there is more to it than that. But let's just look at that part of that verse for a moment, because it is tremendously important. *The only thing that counts is faith expressing itself through love.* That's the one thing that matters most! If we have faith, but we do not love people, it's nothing! If we have faith, but are not expressing it, what good is it? If we have faith but are not faithful, we might as well not have it at all.

Luckily, there is no test. There's nothing to pass. There's no landmark, benchmark, or mile marker that we have to cross before we can get started. That's not how faith works. We're allowed to get started wherever we are.

Most of you reading this book already have a faith of some sort. That's excellent. We have things that we believe, we've put our trust in Jesus, and we think the world needs more of Him. One could say that we have faith.

Now, it's time to go from faith to faithful.

It's time to put our faith into action. It's time for us to express our faith through love to the world. Because if the world isn't getting more Jesus because of us, it doesn't really matter what we believe.

Some of us don't feel qualified to express our faith. Some of us feel like we don't have enough answers to live it out. And some of us are honest, and just don't feel like loving someone all the time. That's okay. That happens to all of us. The point though is that we have to get back at it, or for some of us, get started.

The thing that matters most is faith being expressed through love. We all have plenty of excuses for not doing it, but none of them are good enough. We didn't pass a class, but we still got the degree. It's time to put our faith on our resume.

Let's get started, shall we?

I Survived The Van Flatulence Of 2002

The Windows Don't Open!

When I was in elementary school, I played soccer. I wasn't especially good (I was one of those kids that had to gain a bunch of weight before he could grow, making me rather slow in the only time in life when it matters if you can run fast), but my friends played, so I played and had a fun time. One of the things I remember about soccer was traveling to games. I particularly liked the rides home, especially if we won. Everyone was dirty and smelly; we'd listen to music, tell jokes, and if the drive was long enough, we'd stop at McDonald's.

There was one ride home that I think I will never forget. I went to a small Christian elementary school, so we didn't have busses; we would just ride in a fifteen passenger van.

And when you take fifteen hot, sweaty, tired children, stuff them with Big Macs, and cram them into a van, occasionally, something tragic will happen. And on this fateful night, it happened.

Somebody ripped a big one.

They let out the tire pressure. They cut the cheese. They practiced some classical butt yodeling. (I'm trying not to say "fart," as this was a swear word in my home growing up). They let one fly, and fly it did. However, this was not a classic comical bowel expression where everyone turns, takes a second, and then responds with either disgust or uproarious laughter. This particular duck stomper was what we call S.B.D. (Silent, But oh so Deadly).

It took a moment for everyone to realize what was happening. But pandemonium quickly ensued. Children screaming. Older boys climbing over the bench seats in an attempt to find fresh air. Those in window seats clawing and scratching desperately to open a window that only opened an inch or two on the bottom. Accusations began flying of who was to blame for this disaster! *It was Tony! It wasn't me! Whoever smelt it dealt it!* Some screamed, some cried, all panicked. My reaction was to dive on the floor under the seat and scream like a maniac until the general pandemonium settled down.

It was a lot of fun.

But there's something you should know about me that makes this part of the story interesting. *I have almost no sense of smell.* I can't smell most things. I can smell really strong smells, and I can smell things when I put them right up to my nose. But on this day in the van, I smelled nothing. I just went along with what everyone else was doing.

(By the way, if you're finding yourself feeling bad for me because I can't smell; don't. I've actually come to see this as a blessing. In my experience it seems that most smells are bad. It seems like people are often commenting on how bad a smell is, but rarely comment on how good it is. The most common good smell I miss out on is coffee, but I can smell my own cup if I bring it up to my nose. So, no, I can't smell garlic bread in the oven, but I also can't really smell a diaper when I'm changing it. So, you know, Yin Yang).

Isn't that strange though? I never smelled anything, but I went along with it. I just pretended. And this is where I will transition into what I really want to discuss in this chapter.

Faking it.

Sometimes, if we don't feel qualified, we still want to look qualified, so we fake our way through it. And this is no more common anywhere than in Christianity.

Show Time

Does this sound familiar?

Sunday morning... showtime.

Hair done? Check.

Clothes cleaned, ironed, and deodorant stain free? Check.

Jewelry? Check.

Kids not fighting? Check.

Spouse looks presentable? Check.

Leather-bound Bible with my name on it and enough wear and tear to imply that I read it often but not so much wear and tear to imply that I don't believe it to be sacred and keep it in quality condition? Check.

Anger, frustration, anxiety, and disappointment from the week suppressed? Check.

Alright, big smiles and everybody hold hands. We only have to pull this off for an hour people. Here we go.

Ahh… church. That special time of the week when we take all of the junk that's happening in our lives and hide if from our closest friends and others that want to help us, because Jesus.

And you thought you were the only one.

Pretending is everywhere, and it takes many different forms. Sometimes, it's subtle, and other times it's obvious. Some are more ambitious with what they fake and blur the line straight into lying, but it's all around us. Some of us dress our families, some use big words, some wear jewelry they can't afford, some volunteer, some pray loudly, and some just stay quiet so nobody knows they don't know the answer.

I don't know how it started, but for some reason, many of us feel the need to have perfected this Christianity thing. And if we haven't perfected it, we feel the need to portray to others that we have, which is strange considering the entire purpose of the church is to help each other strive for Christlikeness. I don't know how it started, but it is a problem.

The Problem With Pretending

Can we just start with how exhausting pretending all the time is? Preparing for situations, making sure everything looks just right, learning the lingo, knowing the right things to say, what to wear, how to act… it's exhausting! No wonder people stop going to church; they don't have the energy to keep it up anymore! It takes a lot of time and energy to fake perfection in church; time and energy that could be used for really great things.

I think the primary concern with a church full of people pretending is that we can no longer get the help that we need because we aren't supposed to need help. If we've fallen into the trap of believing that we are supposed to have everything figured out, then we can't ask for help, because we would have to admit that we don't have it figured out. (Which is super ironic because, supposedly, we're surrounded by people who know exactly how to help us because they have it figured out and we don't). It's a vicious cycle.

So, suddenly, we have a church full of people saying things like,

Oh no, I never yell at my kids!

Porn? Never touch the stuff myself.

I never gossip, you know who does though…

No, that class isn't for us. Our marriage is really solid.

I really never doubt anything I believe.

We bought the car with cash. Debt isn't an issue for us.

We have buildings full of people who need, and even want, help. And in that same room are others who need help with the same thing. And in that same room are people who could *actually help them*. And yet, we all sit in our pews, try not to crease our pants, sing as loud as we can, shake hands, and go back home.

The real tragedy of this is that we stop growing. If we're committed to looking like we've already attained perfection, and we've already accomplished our goals, then we cannot take the steps we need to take in order to grow. We can't ask for help when we're struggling because that would blow our cover. We can't ask the question we want to because we're supposed to already have the answer. We can't admit that we're struggling because we think nobody else is.

Instead of trying to get better, we settle for pretending to already be there.

Amazing Perfection

What's really hilarious about all of this is on any given Sunday we use, and overuse, the very solution to this problem.

Grace.

We love to talk about it, don't we?

Amazing Grace

God's perfect grace

Saved by grace

His grace is sufficient for me

Your grace is enough

If God is so Ding-Dang gracious, why are we pretending to be perfect!?

Why do we feel the need to fake perfection when our God's perfect forgiveness and grace are the very cornerstones of

Christianity? We all know we need God's grace; we all know that everyone need's God's grace. Why on earth then are we pretending to be the only ones!? Do we honestly think that everyone else has it all together? Do we really think *all of that grace* is just for us?

It's not. And we're not the only ones that need it. We're not the only ones who are pretending to have it all figured out. None of us are perfect. None of us are qualified. And that's okay. I think the truth is that we want to be qualified to serve God, but we've fallen into the trap that being qualified means attaining perfection. I think a huge reason that we think we need to be perfect is that we're surrounded by other people pretending to be perfect. So, rather than start where we are, we fake it. We try to blend in. Because if we're perfect, then we're qualified.

And this completely misses the point. We are where we are for a reason, even if it doesn't seem good enough. God has a plan for us right where we are, but we can't do it if we're pretending to be done.

It's going to start with one of us being really brave. It's going to start with a few of us being willing to say *I don't have it all figured out. And some of my junk is dark.* It's going to start with a few close and trusted friends, but it will lead to others finally being able to say *me too.* It will lead to others saying *we can help.* Once we're not pretending to be perfect, we can start working on being better.

So the next time we're confronted with the choice to be honest or fake, I hope we'll choose honest. I hope we'll just admit that we don't smell anything.

Weekly Forced Social Interaction

Wow, you guys sound great! It's been amazing singing with you, why don't you turn to the people around you and make them feel welcomed!

Ahh, yes. Greeting time in church. Everyone's favorite weekly forced social interaction. Time to shake hands with complete strangers and forget their names instantaneously. Or better yet, shake hands with people we've known for years and make them feel welcome in their church.

Look, I'll just say it, I don't really like this time in church.

I think I get the point; make visitors feel like they belong and encourage a sense of community in the church, but I don't think this twenty second hand shaking ceremony accomplishes that goal. Maybe I'm just too cynical to function, but I don't think I'm alone in this. However, it doesn't seem to be going anywhere, so here are my tips on getting through the awkward greeting time like a pro.

Hand Courtesy

Let's start by talking about hand courtesy. (I'm looking at you sweaty hands guy).

Honestly, is there anything grosser in the world than grabbing a sweaty hand? (Gag). It's just yucky. And honestly, can someone truly make you feel welcome if their hands are sweaty? *Why are they so sweaty? Are they sick? Are they nervous? Is something about to happen?* If you have sweaty hands (and you know who you are) just wipe them off beforehand, or go in for the hug. A hug from a stranger is better than a sweaty handshake from a stranger.

Next on hand courtesy is lotions and hand sanitizers.

Don't put lotion on your hands right before the hand-shaking time. It makes your hands all sticky and clammy (Two adjectives that are bad in any context), and then I don't know why my hands smell like cucumber melon all day. Just wait until after for the lotion, and at least, wait a few minutes before applying the hand sanitizer. We can all smell it, and we all think you're putting it on because of us.

Finally, with hand courtesy, make sure your hands are germ-free.

Look, if you sneeze during the greeting time, just don't expect to be greeted that day. If you see someone sneeze, you don't have to greet them, okay? They'll be fine. They'll make other friends, and they can all just stand over in the corner and sneeze all over each other. Don't worry about being rude or impolite. The rude part is extending a snot-ridden hand, not refusing to grab it.

So, now that our hands are dry and clean; let's move on.

Speaking Of Greeting

What should you say? This can be trickier than it seems. It's easy to get tongue-tied and trip over a few greetings, or use one that results in a response that you weren't ready for. So, try to plan ahead of time what your opening line is going to be. The easiest thing to do, when it's an option, is to just repeat back whatever they say.

> "Good morning!"
> "Good morning."

Simple, elegant, and effective. But timing here is critical. Don't let more than a moment or two pass while waiting for someone else to start, because then, you're just both looking at each other and not speaking, which doesn't make anyone feel welcome anywhere. So, if they don't start, you'll have to lead.

The best thing to do in this situation is to use statements rather than questions.

> "Hello!"
> "Nice to see you."
> "Happy Day."

Try to avoid open-ended questions, especially if you don't actually want the answer. We can just be honest here for a moment and say, there's that one person in every church we don't ask open-ended questions to because the answer will be long and uncomfortable.

> "How are you?" *Wait. No!! I didn't mean it!*
> "Oh, well, thank you for asking, not so great actually. You know, the squirrels are back again, and I think this time they are specifically targeting my cucumbers…and we caught Jeremy trying to steal fish from the pet store again…and did I tell you about the sore on my…"
> "Yesyesyes, you did. You totally did already tell me about that, and I wish I had time to hear about it again, it's just that the next song already started… So…bye."

We've all been there.

So, if you don't have time for the answer, or don't want the answer, stick with statements of fact, and brief greetings. (Pro-tip: check what time it is. If you have an afternoon service, you don't want to walk in and say good morning. It just throws everybody off).

A final note on what to say, please, don't try to initiate something scripted unless everyone is doing it. Don't try to throw in a *He is risen* in the middle of July, or *peace be with you* unless someone else says it first. Keep it as simple as possible, let them lead if you can, or use direct statements.

Who To Greet

Let's talk briefly about who you should greet. There are often a lot of people, and you're not going to get to all of them. Everyone should be greeted, but nobody wants to be greeted by 45 people. So, who should you greet?

Let's start with how far you should travel to greet someone. I think a good rule is greeting your aisle; turning around being optional. You don't need to run to the back of the auditorium to make sure you greet everyone. You don't need to climb over chairs to greet the next aisle. Just greet those nearby.

First-time visitors can be trickier. We want to make sure they feel welcome, but you don't want to be the person scanning the room for visitors like a big game hunter. *Wait…is that?… It is! That's a visitor!*

And then just start throwing people out of your way to get to them. *Move! You don't matter Cheryl!*

Just get the people in your general vicinity.

(A quick note on that, we've all been tempted to greet the people we came with.

> "Hi, my name is Archibald!"
> "I know who you are, we've known each other since the third grade!"

It's not funny. It's never been funny. Please avoid this at all costs).

Now, sometimes, it can be tricky to know when to sit back down. These things can go on for a while, and every church lets it run for different amounts of time. Basically, you just don't want to be the first one to sit down. You don't want the person in front of you to turn and find you already seated, and then have to explain how you thought we were done with hand-shaking, and then stand back up, only to be asked to be seated moments later. If you're done shaking hands, but nobody else has sat down yet, just stand there awkwardly. It's okay; we're all doing it.

And finally, I feel like I shouldn't have to say this, but this is not the time for pickup lines. This greeting time is not sponsored by Christian Mingle. This is not the time to go and meet the new girl or try to make sure the new guy feels welcome. Okay? God did not bring the two of you together during the greeting time.

You're just going to have to wait for the summer mission trip to fall in love like everybody else.

So, there are my tips for getting through this trying time in our lives. Maybe someday, we'll just stop doing it, but there are a lot of things we might stop doing someday. So, until then, turn to your neighbor and make them feel welcome.

And then immediately, apply hand sanitizer during the prayer.

Nobody Actually Likes Swimming

Who Is Bringing Coinage To The Pool?

I was on the swim team at my local pool for most of middle and high school. Why I did this, I have no idea. Honestly, the idea of getting really good at swimming is just silly to me. I really don't know when people think this is going to come in handy. I suppose if you are regularly chased by sharks, then you should try to get really good at swimming. But if that's the case, you should really just reevaluate some of your life decisions. Or get a harpoon gun. That sounds way more fun (And effective).

I participated on the swim team because all of my friends were on it. I didn't actually like swimming, but I did like refusing to swim, mastering the art of looking like I was swimming while actually just walking along the bottom, making up my own swim strokes, getting out of the pool and telling everyone else to swim faster, and horsing around in the water. It was fun to be on the swim team. But the actual swimming? I have only one word to describe swimming competitively.

Boring.

Boring! So boring! You spend hours staring at the bottom of the pool, or even worse, the sky. Your only hope is that somebody dropped a penny or something in the pool, so you, at least, have something to look forward to every lap. There's nothing to see, you can't hear a thing, and you can't even interact with each other when you swim by, because you're both under-water! It is so dreadfully boring, on top of being excruciatingly physically difficult.

And if the swimming part isn't bad enough, the big reward for all of your work is going to a swim meet. Hooray! You mean now I get to swim in a tiny little-swim suit in front of a lot of people for one minute, and then watch other people swim? Sign me up! Perhaps the only thing more boring than swimming itself is watching other people swim. Sure, we would cheer like crazy for our teammates in the pool, but it didn't matter. They can't hear you! They're under water! Honestly, it's a silly activity to participate in, and I would encourage you to enjoy swimming for what it was intended for: leisure, and retrieving stuck fishing lures.

I tell you all of this because it helps to illustrate just how much I admire Olympic swimmers.

Not only do I understand more than most just how impressive what they are doing is, and how fast it is, and how hard it is, I also understand just how mind-numbingly boring what they have to do to get to that point is. I can somewhat understand just how terrible the life of an Olympic swimmer really must be.

Their days start off early (I assume). They start with an alarm going off at 5:00 telling them it is time to get up and eat something horrible. Probably a green smoothie (Congratulations on drinking salad for breakfast. That's gross. Breakfast should never be green) or something involving egg whites. Then it's time to get changed, and head to the pool. The cold pool. It's time to take off warm, comfortable sweatpants and jump into a cold pool at 5:30 to start a day filled with the most agonizingly boring physical activity known to mankind. The reward for which will be being sore, tired, and super hungry.

This is not living. This is survival at best. And yet they do it. Every day.

My Goal Is To Get Out Of This Pool

This is genuinely amazing to me. What's so impressive about this is our athlete's ability to focus on their goal. Olympic athletes have to set crazy long-term goals and stay focused on them for years. This is wild to me. I'm pretty good at focusing on my goals, but I'm much more of a short-term goal kind of person. Like, I'll set the goal; to not be watching Netflix in two hours. That's a realistic goal for me. It's short-term, measurable, and simple.

Maybe you're like me, and the idea of a multiple yearlong goal sounds really intense. Maybe you're like me, and you are super good at setting goals. You've set goals to get organized, lose weight, read more, learn languages, cook better, parent differently, vacation more...you and me. I can set goals with the best of them. It's the accomplishing part that's impressive. It's the jumping in the pool on a Thursday that gets really hard.

Do you think, maybe, just maybe, there are some days where our Olympic swimmer wakes up and says something like this?

"You know what? I do not feel like waking up today. I feel like turning off this stupid alarm, pulling the blankets up and drifting in and out of sleep for the next two hours. Then I think I'll ease into the morning. Make my way to the kitchen. Make my green smoothie. Pour that smoothie down the drain. Make some coffee and something involving bacon and cheese for breakfast. Cuddle onto the couch and binge watch Parks and Recreation on Netflix."

Now that, is living.

But they don't do it. Why? And How? And again, why?

Because they have a goal, and they have figured out how to chase after it with everything in them. They are completely and totally committed to their goal. It doesn't matter what they have to sacrifice. It doesn't matter how they feel that day. It doesn't matter. They have a goal, and everything in their life is pointing them toward that goal.

We can take a lot away from this example. I think the thing that sticks out most to me is the dedication to their goal, and what that should look like in our lives. Each one of us should be that dedicated to something. And I believe that thing should be Jesus. I think every one of us should be chasing after Jesus with that same level of intensity, where it doesn't matter what we have to miss out on. It doesn't matter if it hurts. It doesn't matter how we feel that day. It doesn't matter what we want in the short-term because we have a long-term goal we're chasing with everything in us.

Our goal is to become more and more like Jesus, until people see him, instead of us.

I really don't think we are called to casually enjoy Jesus. I just don't think that's how it works. For starters, I don't think you can truly meet Jesus and not be completely and totally obsessed. (He's just so cool). But that's also not what he asked of us. He said wild things like *Deny yourself, Pick up your cross* and *Follow Me*.

These are not casual commands. These are not things that come easily or naturally. These are commands that take daily commitment.

I love how Paul talks about chasing after his goal. He talks about his old life, his life before his goal, being crucified with Christ. *That part of his life is dead.* If anyone knew how to get after a goal, it was Paul. He chased Jesus until it killed him. Everything he did was pointing toward his goal. Every decision, every step, every word, was all trying to get closer, trying to introduce people to Jesus.

Our Olympic swimmers don't take days off because that part of their lives is dead! The life they lived before their goal is gone, and we have to be the same way with our faith. Our life, before we set a new goal, is dead.

We Like Floating, Drinking, Tanning, and Surviving

Lots of people casually enjoy swimming, and that's fine. It's not fine how many of us casually enjoy our faith. That's just not what we're supposed to do. Even without the Bible, and Jesus' words to us about following him, doesn't something inside you want to chase after a goal like an Olympic athlete? Isn't it inspiring? Isn't there just an in-born desire to follow Jesus and not let anything stop you? Don't you just feel called to it?

I don't think anyone feels called to be lukewarm. Lukewarm is a word the Bible uses to describe a faith that is half-hearted. It exists, but it's not all in, it's not committed to a goal. Lukewarm is like the swimmer that never places. They work kind of hard, they would like a medal, they like the idea of swimming, but they're not truly committed. When something better comes along, they go after that. When practice gets hard, they quit early. Their goal exists, they could tell it to you if you asked them, but they're not truly committed.

That can't be us in our faith.

But I get it. Sometimes, it gets really hard. (Please don't for a moment imagine that I don't think it gets hard). How do we chase after our goal when it gets hard? How do we stay focused when we would rather sleep in, eat junk, and watch Netflix? I think there's one more lesson we can learn from our Olympic athlete.

They surround themselves with people and things that are pointing them toward their goal.

Everything in their life is pointing them toward their goal. The schedule they maintain keeps them focused. The food they eat nourishes their body for the intense workouts. The workouts themselves strengthen, and prepare them for the competition. They surround themselves with coaches, trainers, and other athletes to push them. They listen to content to make them better. They read, watch, listen, hang out with, research, and pay attention to people and things that are moving them in the direction of their goal.

And this is exactly what we need to do—we have to fill our lives with people and things that are moving us toward our goal. So, we surround ourselves with people that are encouraging and on the same journey. We consume content through the internet, television and books that help us stay focused. We fill our homes with meditation, conversations, and worship. We surround ourselves with things moving us toward our goal so that we're always moving toward the goal.

And then, we remove things that are moving us in the wrong direction. Just like with any goal, there are things that need to go. If we want to lose weight, we don't keep ice cream in the freezer. If we want to read more, we don't upgrade our cable package. If we want to cook more, we don't clip restaurant coupons. And if we want to become more like Jesus, we need to make some cuts too. I don't need to list them for you. You know what's keeping you from your goal. Get rid of them.

So, let's set a goal. A crazy goal. A long-term goal to be more and more and more and more like Jesus. Let's take our faith to Olympic levels. I don't think any of you want to have a casual faith. I just don't think that's inborn in any of us. I think we all want to be all in.

Let's get up early, fill up on what we need, and dive in.

The Time I Participated In A Mandatory Fitness Assessment

Ripped Like Abe

Do you remember the Presidential Fitness Test? (I'm not sure if that's what it was officially called or is called anymore, but that's what we called it). It was the strangest thing. Every year, for like two weeks, gym class would be nothing but waiting for your turn to do some kind of physical challenge. As I recall, there were five events:

Push-ups/sit-ups,

Pull-ups/bar hang,

Shuttle run,

One mile run,

And the V-sit and reach.

It was intense, challenging, and above all else, boring.

As an adult, it's easy to look at these things and say, *Who cares?* But as a child, and certainly as a male child, these things mattered as much as anything else had ever mattered in our lives. One of the highest honors that could be bestowed on a ten-year-old boy was the coveted *Presidential Level* award given to those who were able to accomplish all five events at the required level. And almost nothing was more demoralizing than receiving the dreaded *Participant* "award" upon completion. (I think there was a middle level as well, maybe it was called *vice presidential?*)

I remember one particular year; I'm pretty sure it was third grade, the time came for the presidential fitness test. The first event was push-ups and sit-ups. This one had never been a challenge for me. Do the necessary number of push-ups in a minute, no problem. Do some sit-ups for a minute after that, still no problem. I passed with soaring colors.

The next meeting was pull-ups and/or bar hang. I couldn't do a pull-up to save my life, but neither could anybody in third grade. Why they made us jump up and try in front of everyone, I don't understand. But luckily, I was able to hang in there just long enough in the bar hang to pass the second trial. So far, no problem.

The third event was the shuttle run. (Remember this one? Run to this line, now run back, now run to the line again, now run back. This has not come up since for me). I remember this particular shuttle run experience because we had two chances. The first time, I didn't make it. I was too slow. So, summoning as much energy and speed as I could, I lined up for my second run. I remember flying through the finish line and turning to hear my gym teacher say that I had made it, *on the dot.* One-tenth of a second slower and I had not made the cut. But a win is a win. I had survived. *Presidential status, here I come.*

The next event was the dreaded mile run. A mile is a really far distance when you're only four feet tall; and in third grade, it might as well have been a Tough Mudder. Everyone was anxious about this one, me in particular, as this had been a difficult event for me in the past. I don't remember much of the race, but I do remember stopping at one point to catch my breath and thinking, *If I lose by a few seconds, I will never forgive myself for taking this break.* I immediately took off at a dead sprint, rounded the final corner, crossed the finish line, and heard my time.

I had made it! Once again, by a narrow margin, but a win is a win. I celebrated with my other friends who had made it this far, and mourned with the others who had been left behind. Only one event left—the V-sit and reach.

This event still seems odd to me, mostly because a device had to be created in order to measure flexibility that did not exist before. In this event, you sat down, straightened your legs, and reached as far past your toes as you could, where a mechanism that looked like a box with a ruler welded to the top measured how flexible you were. So, I sat down, straightened out and reached. It was only then that I realized something strange.

I could barely reach the measuring stick! Like, even the very end of it, let alone the Presidential mark that now seemed lightyears away! I couldn't do it. These new third grade muscles that allowed me to run so fast and push so hard… were really inflexible. I was nine; I had never stretched before! And therefore, failed to reach my goal. I was a participant. Nothing more.

The next week, our teacher handed out the results. We each received a piece of paper (cardstock with a real presidential seal stamped in the corner and everything) dictating how we did. I knew the results, but when you're a child, you'll get your hopes up for anything. So, I hoped and hoped that somehow they understood, and I would still be awarded the *Presidential Level* of fitness. I received my paper. Flipped it over. And read the words;

ANDY BUCKWALTER
PARTICIPANT

I was furious. I grabbed the paper, crumpled it into a ball, and threw it away. For which, I was reprimanded by my teacher. (Something about being ungrateful, someone took the time to make that…whatever. I tried and failed, and as a man, I needed to break something). I was so frustrated. Why would anyone want a paper indicating that they participated in a *mandatory* fitness assessment? It was an insult. But worse than that, it was a reminder that I had failed.

What The Paper Didn't Know

Now, here's the funny thing about all of this. I was a really athletic kid! I played all of the sports either with my friends or in an organized fashion. I was never picked last; I usually scored a goal, touchdown, or a run. I was decently fast, strong, and knew the strategy for each game. I even did pretty well at the presidential fitness test! I passed all of the demanding exercise oriented events! The only one I couldn't do involved sitting down and only took ten seconds. I knew I was physically fit, and my friends and family knew it as well, but on that day, I was told that I was not. And I believed it.

Isn't it strange how we allow someone else's standard to determine how we think we are doing? There is another word that we use to describe this phenomenon: *Comparison*. Yes, comparison, the opposite of contentment, the destroyer of satisfied, the "make you feel lousy because of someone else" thing.

This happens in our lives all of the time though, doesn't it? We feel pretty good about ourselves until we go to the gym and hear what a personal trainer thinks we should look like. We think the house is clean until our mother-in-law comes over. We're happy with our grades until someone tells us the average. We like a picture of ourselves until we see an Instagram model wearing the same shirt. We're happy with our marriage until we double date with the Johnsons.

And then there's parenting. Quick rant and then I'll get back to the point.

It can be a scary time to be a parent right now. We live in a time where unsolicited parenting advice is totally acceptable to hand out for some reason. There are blogs dedicated to nothing but showing how other parents are doing a bad job. There are things called organic, BPA is a thing, gluten is bad now, potty training has rules, this bottle is better than that one, you're supposed to discipline your kids, but never in public… and virtually every one of these is completely and totally based on opinion. I have the luxury of being the kind of person that *genuinely* does not care how you think I should raise my children. But if you're someone who has a difficult time with other people's standards? This can be honestly terrifying.

Mom-shaming is an actual word that people use in sentences. We live in a world where one person's opinion has the power to set a standard for someone less confident (note: not less informed) than them. Social media, the internet, and the news are all full of new standards being set for parents every day, and most of them are absolute non-sense. Honestly, if we would get off our phones and computers and stop letting our standards be set by other people, we would be perfectly content with how we're doing as parents and would raise the kinds of children we want to see.

Okay. I'm done yelling about parenting.

Comparison is so prevalent in our lives that we don't even notice it anymore. We compare everything. It's like we don't know how to be happy unless we know we're doing something better than someone else. And we know we shouldn't be happy if someone is doing it better.

Allowing our standards to be manipulated by someone else can happen in any area of our lives, and church is not excluded. How we should dress, what we should read, shows we should watch, events we should attend, which church to go to, how we should speak…There are rules that people will make up. And if we allow ourselves, we'll start comparing ourselves to their beliefs and rules.

We're happy until someone says, *You know, you really shouldn't…* or, *You know, you really should…*

Their motivation may be in the right place; it may not be; it doesn't really matter. What matters is how we respond to this information. People will set standards that aren't ours. We'll be tempted to compare ourselves to other people. The problem isn't that other people exist, or that they have their own standard, the problem is when we start to think we are less because of this. And this is especially tragic in our relationship with Jesus.

Survey Says... Nobody!

It's easy to start to think that we should be reading the Bible or volunteering more, or we should be leading by now, or we should pray like them, dress like them, be as knowledgeable as them, be as close to Jesus as them. But that's so far away from the point. The point is to have a relationship with Jesus. *Our* relationship with Jesus. *Your* relationship with Jesus.

I always think it's strange when relationships are compared. It happens all the time. You can blame social media for making relationships look perfect if you want, but we're the ones who believe it. *They look so happy, they probably never fight. I bet he buys her flowers. I bet she cooks dinner every night. I bet their sex life is amazing. They look like they communicate so well. They're always smiling at each other...* This is odd to me.

Comparing things like six-pack abs, mustaches, and cars makes sense to me, but relationships? I don't get it. I have a relationship, and I'm happy with it. Maybe they do things differently than we do, that's ok with me. Maybe they've been at it longer than us, that's ok with me too. They may have deeper, longer, more meaningful conversations than we do. So what? I like the time we spend together. I like our conversations. I like where we are. Did you catch that?

I like where we are.

Of course, we should want to get better. We should always want to get better, in every area of our lives, but not because we're comparing ourselves to someone else! This next part is important, so I'm going to put it in its own line and write it in italics.

Jesus is not comparing us to anyone.

And now, I'll repeat it for emphasis. Jesus is not comparing us to anyone! That's all us! We're the ones looking at other people to see how we're doing. We're the ones listening to other people instead of Jesus. We're the ones allowing ourselves to believe that we should be or shouldn't be. That's not Jesus! Yes, Jesus is pulling us toward him; yes Jesus wants us to be better; yes, there are areas in our lives that need change and improvement, because he's comparing us to HIM! He wants us to look like HIM! Jesus is not comparing us to other people. Jesus is not comparing our relationship with him to other people's relationship with him.

Jesus likes where we are. He likes where you are. You're supposed to be here. Maybe you want to pray more, that's great! But only if you want it for you and Jesus. Not because someone else prays more. Not because someone else thinks you should.

I was an athletic kid, and I knew I was athletic. I could very well have gotten the participation award, put it in my backpack and said *I know I'm athletic even if this paper doesn't think so.* The paper was wrong, but it had power over me because I believed it. And the same is true of comparison. It only matters if we believe it.

So, enough with the comparison. Enough with looking at others to see how we're doing. Enough with basing our worth on other people's accomplishments. We're exactly where we need to be, as long as we're moving toward Jesus. It doesn't matter what trophies and awards other people have. A relationship with Jesus is the one place where I definitely want a participation award.

We Can Do Better Than This

There are things that happen in this world that there is no need for.

Things like jeggings.

Deconstructed food.

The man bun.

Brand name water.

Things that we're just better than. Or we should be anyway. So I thought we could use a chapter to laugh about some things that happen to us where we're left saying, *We can do better than this.*

Doors

Ok, so we're walking up to a set of double doors. Both are available, and you're not sure which one to use, so you decide it's a matter of personal preference, and use the left door... Guys, we can do better than this. There is no need for us to be running into each other whilst entering and exiting buildings.

I sure do hope we both try to use the same door so we can run into each other! Maybe then, I can be forced to wait for this person to leave a building, so I don't get hit with a door. Hopefully, I have my stroller with me!

The correct answer is the door on our right side. That is the correct answer. Even if someone is holding the left door open for us, we open the one on the right and use it. We live in a society based on keeping to the right, why would this suddenly become optional because we added movable walls? It shouldn't. And it doesn't. So, we use the right door.

And by that, I mean the correct door.

Which is also the right door.

Music?

Ok, so now we're at the beach. And someone decides, *I'm going to listen to music that I like. And I like hippy dippy top hits pounding bass drum auto-tune "going to the club and buying bottles" radio nonsense music. I think I'll play it loudly because everybody can appreciate this kind of "music".*

We can do better than this.

Please. We don't want to listen to your noise. We come to the beach to not hear noise. We want to hear the ocean, lifeguard whistles, crying children, fighting couples, bros playing volleyball, and parents yelling at children to come in-to shallower water. These are the noises we crave, not Lil Whoever. Just let me sit here in the "silence" and read until I fall asleep. There will be plenty of time for you to make noise after the sun goes down.

(This also applies to red lights, waiting areas, parks, libraries, neighborhoods, your driveway, and pretty much anywhere other people could hear your music).

I'ma Let You Finish That Word

Ok, so you've decided you're going to talk to me. And you come across a word that has more than two syllables in it. And you decide you're only going to say the first few syllables to me to save you some time.

Friend. You can do better than this.

I feel like I shouldn't have to say that this is not okay—that sandwich is not *delish*, the idea is not *bril*, and your outfit is not *perf*. I genuinely mourn for a society that believes this is an acceptable way to speak to each other. We sound silly when we do this, and we can do better than silly. Not to mention, it won't save us any time. Trust me, the tirade I will immediately launch into will take up far more time than the extra syllable you eliminated would have.

Toilet Paper Panic

Ok, so you're putting a new role of toilet paper onto the dispenser thing, and you think, *There is a right way, and a wrong way to put toilet paper on the dispenser thing.*

(For example; "It goes over! Not under!")

Are we really not better than this? Why is this a conversation people are having? It's toilet paper. This cannot matter. No matter how much we want it to, this cannot matter. There is no right. There is no wrong. Honestly, it's much more concerning to me if this matters to someone than which way the toilet paper goes. Are you not getting toilet paper fast enough? Have you had multiple directional toilet paper crises in your life that lead you to become an advocate for toilet paper installation? Because you should probably see a doctor.

The bathroom is such a great place to think. Let's not waste the opportunity to sit and ponder life uninterrupted on toilet tissue. (By the way, it goes under, not over).

I Was Enjoying That Silence

Ok, so we're at like a dinner party, or we're eating snacks with our friends and there's a moment of silence, and you think about saying, *The food must surely be good because nobody's talking!* Or *well I guess we were hungry because nobody's talking*!

Guys. We're better than this.

Yeah, the food came out, and we all took a bite at the same time. Thank goodness there's silence! The alternative is a group of people talking with their mouths full. Gross. Just because you're uncomfortable with silence does not mean it is time to fill this silence with cliché nonsense.

By the way, some of us were enjoying that silence. Some of us don't believe in awkward silence. We believe only in *glorious* silence. (We fall into one of two categories: Introverts and Parents). It's going to be ok. Soon the chewing will become staggered, and conversation will recommence. Just relax and have some more bean dip.

Spoilers McGee

Ok, so we're talking about a television show we both watch. And you want to know where I am in the show. So you ask, *Are you to the part where Cassandra gets murdered by Calliope...?*

Well, I wasn't. But I am now. So thanks for that. We're better than this. Just ask where I am without prompts. I'll be able to fill you in.

Everybody Loves Fluffy

Ok, so you're sending out a Christmas card, or you're picking out tiny stick figure people to put on the back of your car, and you think, *Well, technically there are seven of us... because of our pets.* Pet owners, we can do better than this.

Why do people think animals are people? It's a dog. It's not people. I'm sure having Jasper around is a lot of fun, but I'm not coming to his birthday party.

I don't know why you let snowball trounce around on your counters, tables, and clothes with her litter infested paws. Maybe *you* like having things batted off your end-tables and finding surprise dead rodents in the middle of the night, but I'm not hanging a picture of her on my Christmas tree. I'm not saying good-night to your guinea pig; I'm not taking a picture with your bird, and I don't want to hear about your turtle's day. Your pets are not people, and I do not love them. Sorry.

(I feel like that came off kind of harsh… Good :) Also, remember making little faces out of punctuation? That was way more fun than emojis.)

Emojis

Listen to me. You are a grown man. We do not need little pictures in our communique. Every great piece of literature, satire, novel, and document was written and communicated without little faces in them. There are so many tools available to us in the English language that allow us to communicate exactly what we mean with nothing but the written word.

This is how adults use words. We can do better than cute Hieroglyphics.

(And heavens to Frank, can we stop with the poop emojis!? Someday, future generations are going to look back and wonder why on earth people were utilizing personified defecation to express themselves. We have to be better than this.) (Don't we?)

It's A Me!

Ok, so we're at an Italian restaurant, and you're speaking. And you decide that when certain words come up, you have an Italian accent. Why? You're better than this. Why do certain words cause you to have an accent? Look, it's perfectly acceptable to say marinara in an American accent. Nobody wants to sit next to the person like, *Yes. I will have the MAURRREENAURRRA sauce, please.* Why this sudden onset accent syndrome sets in from time to time, I don't know.

But we should really have the same accent for all words in a sentence.

I'm Eating This

Ok, so we're eating together. And you decide to tell me that what I'm eating is bad for me… We're better than this guys. What do you think you know that I don't know? Obviously, I know. It's not like I'm just like, *Oh heavens! I thought this was broccoli! How did this Big Mac get in my hand!?*

(By the way, can we stop pretending we don't like McDonald's? One cannot build a franchise on every corner of every city without a customer base. I love it. You love it. Let's stop the McDonald's shaming).

I know it's bad. I don't care.

Enjoy your kale over there.

A Clown In The Rain

Nothing Irrational About It

We all have some irrational fears in our lives. The odds are pretty good that you're afraid of snakes, spiders, heights, bugs, the dark, or mice. Now, some of those can hurt us, but in most cases, none of them will. We don't really know why we're afraid of these things, we just kind of are. Personally, I'm afraid of several of these, but the one that stands out the most is spiders.

Now, this is irrational for several reasons. One, there are no poisonous spiders where I live, so, it's not like I'm in any danger from these tiny little creatures. But also, I'm not walking up to spiders, taking a picture of them, Googling them, and then deciding whether I'm afraid or not based on if they're dangerous. I just see one, and immediately wish I owned a shotgun because I don't have a big enough magazine handy to crush this intruder. (It's something about the way they move that just creeps me out. Seriously, why are they so fast?) But it's irrational. There's no reason for me to be afraid of these bugs (arachnids?).

My second fear is more grounded.

Clowns.

I know that got an amen from some of you. Yup, clowns, the most evil of the children's party entertainers. I don't know what it is about clowns, but I don't like them. What's with the smile painted on? Nobody's happy all the time, just smile or don't smile. Once an emotion is painted on, it's not trustworthy, and I don't like it. Now, let me tell you about one of my least favorite encounters with a clown.

When I was in high school, I ran every day after school. So, one day I'm on my run and at the top of a hill, far too close to my house, across the street, is a clown. Just standing there; holding balloons, (Not kidding) and looking at me. This is not a bus stop or a place people generally congregate. There was nobody else around. There was no reason for it to be there. And on this particular day, it was raining.

Friends, if you encounter a clown in the rain, it's up to no good.

There was no birthday party, no circus, nobody else with it. Just a clown in the rain, standing there with a menacing smile painted on its face. I start the following mental checklist immediately; *did the clown see me? How do I get home from here? Do I have any weapons? Can I best this clown in a physical contest? Could the clown know where I live? How does one defeat a clown? Is it a silver bullet? Or is this more of a wooden stake through the heart situation?* All of this, as I'm running *toward the clown.*

I get to the intersection where it's standing, turn, and run as fast as I've ever run along my path, looking over my shoulder the entire way. It doesn't follow me, which was almost worse. You know when there's a spider in the house, but you lose visual contact? Same feeling.

I get home, burst through the door and yell, "Ma! Is there a clown in this house!?"

Of course, my mother is confused by this question, and perhaps even more confused as I start running through the house with my baseball bat searching for clowns in closets, under beds, and behind doors. No joke, I'm going through the house systematically throwing open doors and raising my bat in the air because I'm sure, there must be a clown hiding in there somewhere, and I have far too much adrenaline and fear coursing through my veins to properly explain myself.

All and all, it was a fun afternoon.

Twelve Grown Men Screaming In A Boat

Fear is a funny thing, isn't it? My behavior was just as irrational as my initial fear. But fear has that effect on us, doesn't it? Sometimes we allow fear to dictate our decisions. Maybe it's in a small way; maybe it's something huge. Maybe we want to go for something, but we're afraid to try—afraid to fail. Maybe we just know we should do something for ourselves, or for someone else. But what will people think? What if it doesn't work out? *What if I get hurt?* If we let it, fear will keep us from doing things we want to do, and even worse, things we need to do.

We haven't looked at many Bible stories in this book, but I want to talk about one of my favorites briefly. Perhaps you've heard that Jesus walked on water. That's cool and all, but that's not really what I want to look at here. I want to look at this story from *inside* the boat.

So, here's the setup;

Jesus sent the disciples away in a boat so that he could pray. (Which by the way, did none of them see a problem with them taking the boat and leaving Jesus? Can't you just hear James, "Jesus, I understand. It's just that, if we take the boat… you won't have it…yes I understand you want to pray…it's just that this is our *only boat*, and if we leave with it…ok, ok, we'll go.") And while they're in the boat, night falls, and a storm hits.

Now, this is not an ordinary storm; these storms got nasty. Like, life-threatening nasty. So, the disciples find themselves in a frightening situation. They're in a boat. It's dark. Like, middle of the sea on a cloudy night dark. The rain is pouring. The wind is whipping violently. The lightning is flashing, and the waves are crashing over the side of the boat. Half the group is probably oaring like crazy, the other half is bailing water out like crazy, and then somebody says, "Hey guys, did you see that?"

And this part is just hilarious to me. Jesus has decided to walk out, on the water, to the boat. Which is really neat…unless you're in the boat.

This is like classic horror movie stuff.

> *The disciples fight the storm in the darkness. As the lightning flashes, something appears hovering over the water—the dark shape of a human.*

"Did you guys see that?" *Deciding it couldn't be anything they ignore it and get back to bailing.*

The lightning flashes, and they see it again. "Dude, I definitely just saw something out there!"

"The lightning's just playing tricks on you, keep paddling!"

The lightning flashes again and the human-shaped creature appears closer.

"Dude, it's getting closer! I'm not even messing with you right now!"

"I saw it that time too!"

"It's a ghost!"

"Get us the (Whoa, this is in the Bible?) out of here! Keep paddling!!"

The lightning flashes again, and it's closer still. The disciples scream in terror!

No joke, my version says they scream in terror! Twelve grown men in a boat, screaming like little girls. This is just so funny to me!

Funny to me, but for these guys, this is one of the most terrifying moments of their lives. It's dark; there's a bad storm; they already think they're going to die, and now, (because, why not?) there's a ghost! This sounds comical, but from inside the boat? Not funny.

Enter Jesus.

Jesus is just always so cool. He walks up, through the storm to these screaming men in a boat and says three things.

It's okay.

I'm here.

Don't be afraid.

The Storm Before The Calm

The story continues, and it gets really good, but I want to stop here because these three statements are so important for us to hear. Jesus walks up to a group of men in a genuinely terrifying situation and says three things. It's okay. *Because I'm here. Don't be afraid.* Don't we forget that? Don't we always forget that? Isn't it easy to look at the storm? Isn't it easy to think there's a ghost? (Or a clown). Don't we forget that no matter what we're going through, Jesus is standing right behind us whispering, *It's alright. I'm here. You don't have to be afraid.*

We have a bad habit of focusing on the storm. If we're honest sometimes, the storm feels all consuming. Maybe we're not in a literal boat in a storm, fighting waves, and fleeing from a ghost. But the fear is still real; the fear is still blinding. It feels like it's all there is.

Just like I acted irrationally when I was afraid, we do the same thing in our lives when fear is calling the shots. Only rather than running through our houses and looking silly, fear has the real capability of hurting us or others. We lash out at a friend. We end the relationship. We lie, we yell, we steal, we cheat. Or maybe we don't do something. We don't speak up. We don't submit our name for the promotion. We don't go to the party. We don't go to the funeral. We don't propose. We don't go for it, whatever it is.

Hearing Jesus' voice over the storm can be really hard. Sometimes, the wind and the thunder are just deafening. The Bible doesn't say it, but it's not impossible that Jesus had to repeat himself a few times before the disciples stopped screaming. And that can be true for us too. I think sometimes, we can't hear his voice over the waves, rain, wind, or our own screaming. But that doesn't mean he isn't there. He's always there whispering: *It's ok. I'm here. Don't be afraid.*

Sometimes, we think that the storm is our guarantee. We think the wind and the thunder are sure things. We think whatever we're afraid of is going to happen, and Jesus might come through for us, when the exact opposite is true. The storm is possible. It might happen. But it might not. And it might not be as bad as we think. But the storm isn't promised. Jesus is. Jesus is guaranteed. We know we *might* hit storms, but we know that we *will* have Jesus.

For some reason, that's hard to remember. I've heard it said that the command, "Do not be afraid" is in the Bible 365 times. (The same number of days in a year for those of you wondering why that is significant). I've never counted, but it seems obvious to me that we're not the only ones dealing with fear in our lives. It seems clear to me that fear is something God takes very seriously, and really wanted us to understand. It's an area we need to be reminded of often.

What are you afraid of? What is it that fear is stopping you from doing? What would you do if you weren't afraid of it? What is the easiest first step you can take towards that goal? If you weren't afraid, what would you do? And what would be the first step? We cannot allow fear to stop us from living out our faith. We cannot allow fear to stop us from expressing our faith in action, and loving people. We just can't.

What if instead of listening to the wind and the thunder, we stopped for a moment to listen for Jesus saying,

It's ok.

I'm here.

Don't be afraid.

What would we do if we really believed Jesus was right there with us? What would we do if we really thought he had our back? Whatever it is, we can't let fear stop us anymore.

Unless it's a clown.

Barbequed Stuffed Animals

Object Lessons And Other Fun Memories

I remember being in youth group. I don't remember how old I was, but I think it was like mid-high school. We were doing a series on talking to our friends about Jesus, and our leaders at the time decided to use a particularly aggressive teaching style for these talks. I remember only two weeks of this series. But I think I shall never forget them.

The first week, we were introduced to an audio track that someone created called "A letter from hell." (This was like fifteen years ago and I still remember the name of it). This audio sample tells a story where a friend of yours dies, is sent to hell, and then gets to send a letter to you. In this letter, they explain how they are terrified, miserable, in agony, and, above all else, furious with you for having never shared your faith with them. There is screaming, the creepiest of music, yelling, blaming, and incredibly vivid storytelling, including a detailed account of our friend begging angels not to throw him into the lake of fire. It concludes with our friend, stating, just before being cast into hell, "…I wish…you were here." In a word, it was… Alarming.

The next week was even better.

We all sit down in a circle. Our leader for the night gets us started by bringing out a stuffed puppy. It was pink and cute, and surprisingly soft. He then says he is going to pass it around and we are each to write the name of one of our friends, who is not saved, on the puppy with markers. We do this. Then another leader takes the stuffed puppy and leaves the room. Then we talk for a little while about why it is important to share our faith with our friends, at which point, I assume the object lesson is nearly at its end; *what if we never see the puppy again, what if that was our last chance…* pick your object lesson.

It is then announced that we are going to go outside. *Outside? Ok that sounds fun.* So, we walk outside together, fairly quietly to where the rest of our leaders are standing around a small charcoal grill. And on the grills of this grill is sitting…the puppy. (Don't get ahead of me). Our leader then says something. Who on earth knows what he said? He could have said anything! It didn't matter, because after he said it, he struck a match, threw it at the puppy on the grill, and it immediately burst into flames.

I. Am Not. Fuhreaking. Kidding You. I was there.

We stood there, probably fifteen of us, in absolute silence and watched a stuffed puppy with the names of our friends on it, burn until it was gone. (Which took longer than anyone thought by the way).

And that boys and girls is why you should talk to your friends about Jesus.

Afterward, I think we went inside and played a game! Like any of us was emotionally prepared for dodgeball after imagining our closest friends being soaked in lighter fluid and barbequed for the third straight week!

What's interesting about this is, I don't recall a massive increase in attendance in our youth group after this demonstration. I don't recall trying to witness to my friends afterward. I do remember feeling guilt and shame for not trying to help them. I remember thinking I should be doing more, but feeling really trapped.

Aggressive Evangelism

I'm not the only person to experience this kind of radical teaching about the importance of saving immortal souls before they're launched into an eternity of misery and torture. The point of these "talks" of course being that we needed to be way more intentional about having conversations about Jesus with our friends, that time was a factor, and that we needed to be more assertive with our faith.

Many of us have learned the importance of sharing our faith with people. Some in less terrifying ways than described above, but many of us have been told that introducing people to Jesus is an important part of what we are called to do. And if you're like me, you learned that you need to make sure these conversations happen and may have even been taught how to bring them up, execute them, and mark one more down for the kingdom.

Many of us were taught ways to introduce people to Jesus in an unnatural and forced way. We were taught tricks and lines like the "Roman road," or, "Why does it say *in God we trust* on money?" Some of us were given tracts to hand out and taught how to relentlessly defend our faith. And some of us were even instructed to go so far as to frighten people and warn them of the eternity they were headed for. *If this airplane were to go down right now, do you know where you would spend your eternity?*

Insert Tina Fey caliber eye roll.

This call to actively try to introduce people to Jesus is what I call aggressive evangelism. The point of aggressive evangelism is to force Jesus into the conversation. At its best, its purpose is to help people by introducing them to Jesus. At its worst, it serves as a measuring stick for "evangelists" to determine how well they are doing.

To me, any evangelism becomes aggressive when the relationship is no longer the priority, and will likely end after the "saving of the soul" portion of the relationship is concluded. Many of us have heard the need for what I call Aggressive Evangelism at some point in our lives.

For much of my life, it felt like a never-ending tug of war match in my head. *Shouldn't I be doing more for my non-Christian friends? What if today is my last chance? But what if I bring it up and they get weird? What if it changes the relationship? But isn't it worth trying? Isn't it worth the risk? Unless me bringing it up actually pushes them away from Jesus! What then? What if I make it worse? What if I miss my chance? What if they got hit by a bus while I was taking all of this time to have this conversation with myself!?*

It can be exhausting, frightening, and overwhelming. Putting this pressure on ourselves really isn't fair, and I don't think it's the point. I absolutely believe introducing people to Jesus is the most important thing we can do in our life, but I think it matters how we do it, and I don't think being aggressive is the solution.

Wish You The Best Of Intentions

Now, I'm sure that those who instructed us in these ways had good intentions. I honestly don't doubt that. But in my experience, aggressive tactics like this do not lead to action. I don't know anyone that was convinced of Jesus' love for them. I don't know anyone that was argued into a relationship with him. I've never honestly heard of one of these tactics working. And even if they do work from time to time, I don't think they are our best option.

I don't think we need to shovel our faith down people's throats. We don't need to trick, argue, or convince someone into a relationship with Jesus. Would we ever try that with any other relationship? Would we ever try to line up an airtight argument about why we are the best option? Would we ever have a pamphlet printed out about a friend we were trying to set someone up with? Would we ever try to scare someone into getting coffee with us? *If you don't date me, you could die alone. I might be your last chance at happiness you know.*

And…swipe left.

Of course, we would never do that! We don't run into relationships because the other option is bad. We run to relationships because the person we want to be with is good! Because we want to be with them! We show the best qualities of ourselves and others when we're starting relationships.

What do these scare tactics even give the people we're talking to? Probably fear, stress, maybe even shame. If anything, they accept what we're selling because they don't want to go to hell, not because they want Jesus. And that's not why we want people to meet Jesus. That's not the best part of Jesus.

Jesus isn't fire insurance.

Jesus is hope! He is love! He is trust! He is everything we need to get through everything this world has become!

I don't think people should meet Jesus because they're afraid. We don't want people to run to Jesus because they're afraid of an angry God that's going to light them on fire. We want people running *toward* Jesus, not *away* from hell. We don't follow God; we don't love Jesus, to get away from consequences. We follow God, we love Jesus, because he loves us. Because it's the best thing for us. Because it's the only perfect love we can find. Jesus is not fire insurance. He's love. And love is never scary. Or forced. It can't be.

Let's Keep This Simple

So, I suppose the question becomes, how do we introduce people to Jesus without being aggressive about it. To me, the answer is pretty simple. *We just love them.* Every once in a while there's a fairly simple answer to a complex question, and this can be one of them. Introducing people to Jesus is as simple as loving them. It can be as simple as demonstrating that Jesus is love. Not scary.

Now, I know that sounds like a broad, avoid the question, kind of answer, but I stand by it. I don't think there is a better way for people to meet Jesus, than for us to show his love to people. So, rather than telling people about the sin they need to stop, we tell them that the sin is already taken care of. Rather than trying to convince people to follow Jesus, we show them what it looks like. Rather than demanding change, we serve and become the change. Jesus' love is absolutely irresistible when it's seen. I honestly believe that.

You don't have to convince somebody into love. It's irresistible.

I think it really comes down to our motivation. I'm sure it's not true for some people, but I can't help but think that the drive behind aggressive evangelism is not love. Think about that honestly. Why do we feel the need to push people to Jesus? Is it because we love them? Or is it out of obligation? Do we just feel like that's what we're supposed to do? Are we trying to help them, or are we really just in it for ourselves?

I think there's a reason we see videos of street evangelists on YouTube and social media. If we're motivated by love, if we're truly trying to introduce someone to Jesus, does it matter if our YouTube subscribers see us do it? Would anyone ever have any other conversation with someone through a megaphone? Is there secretly a degree of pride in being able to argue a point better than the other person? Is there a matter of power involved in being able to convince someone to believe something?

Here's the thing guys, if our motivation is to love this person, we really can't screw it up. If our goal is to scratch another notch on our spiritual belt or show people how well we can argue, or how smart we are…yeah, we can mess this up pretty badly. We can even do more damage than good if we're not careful, and we're not regularly checking our motivation.

I don't think we have to push people toward Jesus. I think he's already pulling them toward him. People don't need to be afraid in order to meet Jesus. Quite the opposite in fact.

So, I think we can leave the shame and guilt of not starting these conversations behind. I think we can forget the tactics and strategies we learned. If we want people to meet Jesus, they need to know they are loved. That's where we come in. We don't need to scare people into following Jesus. He's irresistible.

So the next time we have a barbecue, let's leave the stuffed animals at home.

Substitute Person

So, there was a stage in my life where I was a part-time youth pastor, and in order to make more money, I started substitute teaching in my local school district. I really enjoyed this time in my life because I got to interact with a lot of students, I had plenty of down time throughout the school day to work on projects, and the pay wasn't terrible. The students really enjoyed my being a sub as well, as I was named "Favorite Substitute" by many students.

The teachers did not like me.

I was not good at being a substitute teacher. For the most part, I would just kind of write the assignment on the board, and let the students do what they wanted. To me, it was not my job to make sure they did what they were supposed to. I am not their mother. If they don't want to do the assignment, fine! Take the zero! I didn't care at all, and I would tell the students as much.

Guys, this is your assignment. Do it. Do not do it. I don't care as long as it's quiet in here.

That was my usual opening line, particularly in high school. Eventually, the teachers figured out that I was doing this (Which to this day, I stand by) and complained to the principal. Honestly, I have no idea what they were expecting of me. There was no training of any kind, and I had no qualifications related to teaching in any way. Anyway, the principal told me I needed to do a better job, so I started pretending to do a better job.

About a week later, I found myself in a real quandary. A math teacher left me an assignment to teach the class. I'll repeat: he wanted me to teach *new material* to the class. (Honestly, it's concerning to me that someone that doesn't see a problem with this, is educating today's youth). Now, at this point in my life, I have not had an algebra class for like, ten years, and even then, I was not good at it! I read the material and had absolutely no idea what it even said. (There were letters in it. I remember there being letters in math. But I do not remember what to do with them).

So, I did the only thing I could think of. I walked right up to the front of the class and taught the lesson! I pretty much just read to them from the math book, and then wrote a bunch of problems on the board that the teacher left.

But get this, HE DIDN'T LEAVE THE ANSWERS!

Halfway through giving the practice problems, I realize I don't know the solutions to these problems, and I have *no* idea how to solve them myself. So, when everyone was done, I asked what they got. They had about twelve different answers... So I just picked one! *Yes, everyone should have gotten 8.5.* (As I pretend it's written on the paper I'm holding.)

It was during this class that I learned my best strategy for subbing. I would just always say I was a different kind of teacher. So, in this particular math class I told the class that I was actually an English teacher, so I would not be able to help them with their homework. *Just write your questions down for your teacher tomorrow.* In English class, I was a Gym teacher. In Social Studies, I was a Science teacher. Then, I would leave a note for the teacher telling them that we were able to get through the material (And I explained it clearly, professionally, and coherently), but the children seemed confused by my stellar explanation and would need a refresher in the morning.

That was my strategy for High School days. Some days, however, I was in the elementary school. I preferred the high school, but there is something fun about elementary school students. They're just wild and fun, and as an added bonus, I understand what they're learning. So, I had more confidence and didn't have to lie as much.

My favorite day in elementary school was in first grade. It was time for reading, so I told them to get out their reading, but one little girl raised her hand.

"Yeah, what's up?" I say as I realize there is a hand in the air. And her response was just amazing.

All she said was, "My momma's single."

I cannot tell you how I responded to that statement, because I have no idea. In my head, I was laughing uncontrollably. Apparently I met the minimum requirements that she and her mother had set up for potential father material.

You never know what you're going to hear at the elementary school. I highly recommend it.

Eventually, I pretty much only got called for gym teacher substitute jobs. I guess they figured out that was pretty much the only thing I was qualified for. Not to imply that gym teachers aren't more qualified than me, but I was tall, athletic, and I had my own whistle. Those were good days. I finally felt confident in what I was saying; I could wear sweatpants, and one gym teacher had a couch in his office, which I definitely did not get paid to take a nap on. (Yes I did).

I tell you these stories mostly to make you laugh, but also to demonstrate that not knowing the answers really isn't all that bad. Sometimes, when we don't know how to do something, we just do it anyway. Or maybe we just fill in for the person who does know what they're doing. And yes, sometimes, we won't do the best job. Sometimes principals will yell at us. Occasionally we will end up in awkward situations where we don't know what to do. But sometimes we actually get to help too.

I got to lead health classes and have really great conversations with students about eating habits, exercise, and even dating. I remember leading an English class in a debate about some fairly complex ethical questions. I got to just sit and laugh with students at lunch-time. I went on a few field trips where we got to make jokes on the bus ride, and see some really neat things. I got to play kickball and dodgeball and football and all kinds of games with students. I also watched so many movies. Like so many. (For those of you who are teachers, this is the correct course of action for substitute assignments).

No, I definitely didn't know how to substitute teach a class, but I did it. And for the most part, I'm really glad I did. It was uncomfortable at times, but it allowed me to do what I really wanted to do, and created some cool opportunities on its own as well. So, maybe find something you don't feel qualified to do and try it anyway. Because if nothing else, when we step out of our comfort zone, we almost always end up with a great story to tell.

And who knows, you may just get somebody's momma's phone number out of it.

Holy

I Ain't Praying For That

Comedian John Crist has a great bit about prayer requests that are too stupid to pray for, and it makes me laugh every time. I'm not going to quote it here, because I don't know if I'm allowed to, but you get the idea. Haven't you had an experience when someone wants to pray for something, or even worse, wants *you* to pray for something, and your only thought is…Really?

You really want me to pray for your cat right now? Cancer is a thing, but yeah, let's lift up the cat. Sorry, no, I'm not going to be doing that. Jesus is a busy guy, lots of prayers to answer. I'm not using one of mine up on your cat. (Seriously, nothing theological about that statement. That's not how I think prayer works. Relax you guys, just relax).

This random thought lead me down a series of thoughts that ended with me really examining my own prayer life. It occurred to me that I had become really casual in my prayer time. I had really bought into the *Jesus is your best bro* mentality, and the *Relationship not religion* movement. There are some good parts to this mentality, but I think it also lacks in some areas. This series of thoughts, coupled with one verse (That I cannot unread), changed everything for me. We'll get to that for sure, but first, let's talk a little about who we are praying to.

The Big Three

God is complicated. Like it or not, he is. We could unpack that statement for the rest of this book, and the rest of our lives if we wanted to, but for now, let's just talk about this idea of the trinity. Three, and also one. God is one god, with three parts, that are only one, and are also only three. The three being Jesus, the Spirit, and the Father/Creator.

I want to talk about this in particular because I think it really speaks to how we think about God and helps us have a better understanding of who God is. Although the idea of three being one is incomprehensible to humans, if we just let that part slide, I think the trinity actually helps us understand some of the characteristics of God better. Like, we couldn't possibly understand just one God that encompasses all that God is, so He broke himself down into more manageable pieces for us. Let's unpack each one, and take a look at how they impact our prayer life.

(But before we do, I'd like to share with you my very favorite way of understanding the trinity. Are you ready? Here it is; *Neapolitan ice cream*. Do you get it? Three separate entities, chocolate, strawberry, vanilla, that make up one ice cream. I forget who introduced me to that; I'm not the genius that came up with it, feel free to use it at your next youth event).

Jesus Is A Friend Of Mine

Let's start with Jesus. (Shouldn't we always?)

Ahh…Jesus. Isn't he just the best? With his robe, and his beard, and his sandals, and his forgiveness, and his big ole smile? I think this is the God we generally default to in prayer. He's the one we pretend to have coffee with. The one we mention in public prayers. I think Jesus is the part of God we envision leaving footprints in the sand while he carries us through the hardest parts of life.

(Side-note, my grandmother had a picture of this hanging in one of their bathrooms with the *Footprints* poem written on it. I thought it was the coolest thing in the world until I learned that quite literally, every Christian in the world had heard this poem, and that I had been inspired by a cliché all these years. Anyway).

We like Jesus. He's really everything we've ever wanted in a God. Self-sacrificing, wise, a gifted storyteller. Jesus is nice. Calm. Approachable. Jesus is our "best friend." Shoot, the man died for you, for crying out loud. He's just so cool. I think this is also the God we imagine has a sense of humor. We're always talking about God having a sense of humor, but we so rarely envision Jesus laughing. I think Jesus is the funny one.

I think Jesus is also the one we ask to help us find our keys when we're running late. I think he's the one we thank for things like flowers, music, and coffee. He's the one we just kind of tell about our day. I think he's the one we feel comfortable getting angry with, and really sharing what we're feeling.

And I think he loves every conversation.

I think this Jesus we've envisioned is a real part of God. I think there is a place for prayers like these, where we're just kind of open, and we're sharing, and it's conversational. It's intimate. It's nice. We get up early, make coffee, and just spend some time with God. I think we tend to think of Jesus when we do this.

I think Jesus represents the parts of God that we teach children to pray to. (He loves the little children after all). I think Jesus is who we pray to before meals and when we go to sleep. These are happy prayers where we usually say thank you. Jesus is who we pray to in front of our kids. Jesus gets a shout-out before and after sermons, at the end of Bible studies, and during transition periods of Sunday services.

I think part of the trouble with this is our prayers can become so routine. I'm not against having specific times that we pray, but don't these prayers sometimes seem scripted? Don't they feel like they've lost some of their significance? Do you sometimes feel like you pray out of obligation? Do we feel any different after these prayers?

Sometimes, I think because we're so comfortable with Jesus, we forget other parts of God. We forget the parts we wouldn't dare be scripted with. The parts that make us a little uncomfortable. (We'll get there soon).

Holy Smokes! I Mean, Ghost!

Then there's the Spirit. This is the one we don't really get. We don't even know how to picture this one, but we know we like this one as well. Nicknamed "The Helper," this facet of God shows up whenever he feels like it. This part of God looks like a lot of things to a lot of people. A lot of us think of this side of God as the convictor (like the one who convicts), or the shamer, or the voice in the back of your header. For some of us, He's the part of God who gets us through tough times and gives us joy. And then some take this part of God so far as to walk on scalding hot fire, throw literal vipers at each other, and fill auditoriums with gold dust and feathers. (Feel free to look any of these up).

If we tend to talk to Jesus casually, we tend to ask of the Spirit, and then "try to hear" what He says. This is the God we're counting on to give us strength, courage, words, patience (sign me up for a double of that one), all of those things. We ask the Spirit to lead us where we should go. To inspire us to do great things. To give us new ideas and a heart for those who need it.

For many of us, the Spirit acts as a vending machine of the fruit of the spirit. We don't really think about him, but he can really come through in a pinch. We like to pray to the Spirit, but I think this is one we tend to go to when we need something.

Before a big test, job interview, football game, or dance recital, we pray to the Spirit for something. This is who we go to when we're afraid, or in need of something. As much as we may not completely understand the Spirit, we like him. He takes care of us, gives us what we need, and helps us take the next step.

Sometimes, we'll ask the Spirit to do things like fall down on us, or fill this place, or set a fire in our souls. All strange phrases we don't really use in regular conversation. I think part of this strange language we use when talking to God's spirit is our lack of understanding of it. Jesus seems pretty clear, but the Spirit? I'm not really sure what I can and can't ask of this one. There's a bit of a mystery to him.

I think we also tend to credit the Spirit for answered prayers. Even if we asked Jesus, we tend to think the Spirit was at work. The Spirit softens peoples' hearts, gives us understanding, and helps us make better decisions.

All in all, we're fairly comfortable talking to the Spirit, and we generally believe when we ask for something, he hears us, and will give us what we need. Our prayers with Him may be a little self-serving, but I still think he tends to enjoy them. And I think we enjoy talking to the Spirit, even if it looks different than when we talk to Jesus.

I Am

And then there's the big guy.

The Father as he's known. The Creator. The Alpha and Omega. This is one we just call "God." This is the God that I really want us to consider in this chapter. I mentioned a verse that changed everything for me, and I'd like to share it with you now.

The verse is found in Isaiah chapter 6; here's what's happening. Isaiah, God's prophet, is given a vision. And in this vision, he gets to see what's happening in heaven. And this vision is just bananas. Here's what he says,

> It was in the year King Uzziah died that I saw the Lord. He was sitting on a lofty throne, and the train of his robe filled the Temple. Attending him were mighty seraphim, each having six wings. With two wings they covered their faces, with two they covered their feet, and with two they flew. They were calling out to each other,
>
> "Holy, holy, holy is the Lord of Heaven's Armies!

The whole earth is filled with his glory!"

Their voices shook the Temple to its foundations, and the entire building was filled with smoke.

So, to recap:

God is seated on a throne

There are Seraphim (angels) flying around Him

The room is filled with smoke

The Seraphim are chanting and singing together so loudly that the *foundations of the temple were beginning to shake*

These Seraphim are hiding their faces from God behind their wings

And they are all crying, "Holy. Holy. Holy is the Lord of Heaven's Armies! The whole earth is filled with his glory!"

Then, after this crazy scene is described the verse that changed my prayer time for quite a while:

"Then I said, "My destruction is sealed, for I am a sinful man and a member of a sinful race. Yet I have seen the King, the LORD Almighty!"

Isaiah sees this God and basically just says...*I'm dead.*

I'm dead! My destruction is sealed! I'm not going to make it out of here alive. This God is so holy; he is so powerful, so perfect, I can't possibly survive being in his presence. He's awestruck. This is a level of holiness he had no idea was even possible. This is holiness outside of the human experience.

And when he sees it, he assumes he won't make it. It's going to kill him.

Isaiah maybe thought he was doing okay, trying his best, but now, having seen this level of holiness, this much power, grandeur and perfection, he knows there's no way he's walking away from that.

Guys, this is the God we pray to.

This is the same one. This is the scene we enter when we go into his presence. When we pray to God, we are speaking to an unapproachable source of holiness. We are speaking to a god whose presence we literally could not handle being in. Even the seraphim flying around him are hiding themselves! They're shielding their faces with their wings and screaming *Holy, Holy, Holy!*

To repeat something three times was to say it is the utmost. There is nothing more. You can use this in your daily life if you like. The next time you have your very favorite meal, you can say it's delicious, delicious, delicious! Meaning, nothing could *ever* taste better. The next time you see a picture perfect-scene in nature of a mountain, or the ocean, you could say it's beautiful, beautiful, beautiful. Nothing could *ever* be more beautiful. And if you ever meet my wife, you'll understand why I call her hot, hot, hot.

It's basically saying; we don't have the words to adequately describe what we're seeing. There is no adjective that is strong enough or does justice to what we're describing. So, to say *Holy, Holy, Holy* is to say that nothing could ever be more holy. God is indescribable with the human language. Holy doesn't begin to describe how holy and magnificent God is. So we're left with the next best thing. *Holy. Holy. Holy.*

To say *Holy, Holy, Holy* is to be dumbfounded. To be speechless. It's to be unable to even articulate a proper sentence. It's to only be able to think of one word and mindlessly blurt it out, from sheer amazement, fear, and awe. It's to look and pause, and stretch out our arms and just try our best to begin to describe what we're seeing as our eyes fill with tears. It's overwhelmed, all consumed, and utterly amazed.

That is the God we pray to.

Enough

It's hard to comprehend God. God is complicated. He's hard to imagine. And it can be tricky to keep in mind the majesty of his presence in our daily prayer life. It can be hard to keep in mind all of God when we're praying. It can be hard to know how to approach a God that is approachable and helpful, yet also unapproachable and holy. It's not quite as simple as Sunday school made it seem.

But we don't have to understand God. We don't have to know what we're doing to shield our face, fall on our knees and just start with *Holy. Holy. Holy.* And if that's as far as we get, that's okay. We just keep repeating it. Just imagining that scene. God on his throne. The angels flying around, guarding themselves from his majesty, singing and shouting until the foundations of the temple begin to shake. Realizing that we can't survive being in his presence. And yet, we are invited to stay. We're invited to take part in what's happening. We're permitted the honor of being allowed to utter, *Holy. Holy. Holy.*

When we recognize just whose presence we are entering, it changes our prayer time. Personally, I have a really hard time bringing my tiny little problems before that God. On that throne. In that scene. I don't imagine one of the living creatures flying up to God and saying, *Why can't I have the promotion I want?* Or *God, help me find my keys* or anything outside of *Holy. Holy. Holy.*

So, maybe start there. We don't have to understand God, but part of expressing our faith is very intimate worship. Find a quiet place. Fall on your knees, and just start with *Holy. Holy. Holy.* And don't worry about getting past that. It's enough.

I think there is a place for all kinds of prayers. I like the prayers we pray to Jesus, and to the Spirit. I do think we should have a close, intimate, personal, friendly relationship with God. But never at the expense of just who we really are praying to. We can't just forget that our God is also seated on a throne, surrounded by angelic beings, who never stop praising him. We can't forget that from time to time, we get the opportunity to take part in what is already happening in heaven. We get to come into his presence. And we get to live through it.

There is a time and place for happy, comfortable prayer. I believe that. But there is also a place for falling down with the rest of heaven and just hoping to stay alive. There's a place for nothing more than,

Holy, Holy, Holy...

Holy, Holy, Holy...

Holy, Holy, Holy...

Laundry, Nail Care, Chinese Food

Classic Carl

So my wife and I were out getting coffee one night on our weekly date night, and we noticed three stores sitting next to each other in the strip mall. There was really nothing significant about these stores, but what stuck out to us was their names.

The first was called *Laundry*.

The second was *Nail Care*.

And the third was *Chinese Food*.

Brilliant.

I love the names of these stores. I love them so much. A lot of times, I see stores that are called something like,

Diversity

StnaP

Baby Eyelash Gender Neutral Clothing Liquidators

And I really just have no idea what they do. (I do know I don't want to go to them). But I don't have to even consider for a moment what *Laundry, Nail Care,* or *Chinese Food* do. Like, can you imagine walking into a store called Chinese Food and asking them what they do? This is marketing at its finest.

I like to imagine one guy owns all three stores. And I also like to imagine that he has a side consulting business where he helps startups decide on the names of their stores. I also imagine his name is Carl.

> **New Business owner**: Sir, we'd like some help figuring out a name for our store.
>
> **Carl:** Sure, I can help you with that. What do you do?
>
> **New Business owner's partner:** We sell furnace filters.
>
> **Carl:** The name of your store is Furnace Filters.
>
> **Narrator:** *The new business owners begin applauding. Slowly at first, then with dawning comprehension as to what they have just witnessed, their applause turns to wild cheering. In all their days, they have never seen such swift and efficient marketing.*

If Every One Was This Honest

The names of these stores makes me wish other stores used the same strategy when selecting names. They're just so honest, and there's something refreshing about that. If everyone did this, we'd be seeing very different store names around here. You need examples? Alright.

Starbucks	*Expensive, Pretentious, Sugar Coffee*
Target	*White Girl Stuff*
Walmart	*Dirty Target*
Home Goods	*Your House Will Never Look Like Joanna Gaines Designed It*
Any Bar	*A Brief Escape from Reality*
Best Buy	*Not Amazon…Yet*
McDonald's	*Technically Food*
Home Depot	*Stuff To Keep In Your Garage*
Cheesecake Factory	*We Know You Already Ate Too Much… But Cheesecake Is In The Name So…*
CVS	*Everything We Sell Is Cheaper At Target. But Our Receipts Are Longer!*
Netflix	*Your Only Plans For The Whole Weekend*

Wouldn't it be great if stores just had signs like these outside their buildings? You'd know exactly what you're in for. No more looking up stores on the internet to see what they're about. No more searching for reviews. You'd just know.

And then I thought, why limit this to stores?

People Signs

Wouldn't it be great if people had signs like these? You would know exactly what you're getting. So, if someone had a "Helpful" sign you would know to ask them for directions. Someone with a "Strong" sign would be great to help you move, but maybe not to help you with dating advice. And someone with a "Boorish, Rude, and Hairy" sign could be avoided altogether. Much like Bill Engvall's classic, "Here's your sign" bit, it would just come in handy to know what you're dealing with before you start interacting with someone.

And then it occurred to me; that does exist! In one strange social interaction, we publicly display one thing about ourselves to total strangers. We introduce ourselves with one word, phrase, picture, or statement.

Bumper stickers!

Bumper stickers are just so strange to me. How they came to be a thing, I have no idea. What was this first person thinking? *You know, at any given time, there are people behind me that know nothing about me...* And the first bumper sticker came to be.

Mostly, what I don't understand about bumper stickers is what I'm supposed to do with this information.

> Oh, you went to the beach, good for you. I'll be sure to bring that up...and you're exiting.

> Oh, you watch *The Walking Dead*, that's creepy. I guess we could talk about that if we run into...and you're driving really fast, and I'll never see you again.

Oh, you're a republican. I guess we could talk politics if we have to at the next rest stop ...which you did not stop at. See you never.

Oh, you ran a half marathon. That's cool, I guess, but I'm passing you now, so, good luck in your next race. (Can we cool it with the 13.1 stickers? We get it; you ran once. You're driving now. Good for you).

Oh, you're a Christian! Awesome, we can talk about... and you just flipped me off.

Is There Going To Be A Point To This Chapter?

The thing about the bumper sticker is that we get to tell somebody *one thing* about ourselves. Just one. What if the church was going to do this? What if we were going to tell people only one thing about us? As Christ followers, what should be our one thing? What is it that we would want people to know about Jesus and us?

For some of us, the answers come very quickly. *Gracious. Loving. Kind. Hopeful. Rescued. Peaceful. Helpful...*these are things we would love to be known for. We'd be happy if we represented Christ by being these things, and maybe some of us are able to do these things individually. Many of us try to represent Christ the best we can in our daily lives. We try to live out the words that we think should represent Christianity.

But then, something interesting happens. We take a whole bunch of people who want to be these things, get them all together, and it doesn't always look like that.

We call this church.

If Christianity was going to have a bumper sticker, it would be the church. The local church is where people find out just what Christians are all about. It's where people get to truly find out what our one thing really is.

It's our storefront.

And this is where it all comes together.

We know how we want to represent Christ, but I can't help but wonder, what Carl would name our churches. The guy who names organizations based on exactly what they do. What would he name your church? Honestly, what would he name it? And would it include any of the words we wanted on our bumper stickers?

I think we would all love if the name of our church included things like *God is love, Hope for the world, Salvation, Social justice, Regular justice, Peace, Hope, Love*…All good things. These are the things we would like to be known for. But honestly, how many of us can really say this is what our church does?

Some of us might have to face the hard reality that our church's official title might not be what we wanted it to be. Things like,

> Group of people who are inwardly focused and get together to sit through some songs and a sermon once per week.
>
> Highly performance oriented congregation of people who don't really touch on the tough issues of life, or the importance of Jesus.
>
> We're doing things the way we've always done them because that's the way we've always done them.
>
> Group of bored obligated people in pews.

It's not what the church set out to be, but somehow, we got here.

We've Never Done That...Good!

I believe the local church is the greatest hope for the world. Really, I do. And I believe that our churches are full of individual people that already know Jesus. I also believe that these people that know Jesus believe that they should, and want to, express their faith through love to their communities and the world.

But for some reason, when we take these individuals and put them in a building with other people like them, we often fall into a complacent, comfortable, non-expressive existence for an hour each week.

And I don't understand why this happens.

It seems to me, if a group of people gets together every week, and they all have the goal of expressing their faith through love, something really neat should happen! People should notice! That should be a big deal. But for many of us, church feels very differently.

What if the names of our churches actually reflected what we do? What if there was an actual physical sign out front that unbiasedly described exactly what was happening inside? Would we want to make changes? Would we start doing things differently? Would we be embarrassed?

What changes would you want to make?

Now, it's not impossible that you're thinking, *Andy. I am not the pastor of my church. I am not in charge of such things. Why then are you presenting these questions to me?* (You're always so formal). Isn't it interesting that some of us don't feel qualified to try and make the changes we need to in our own church?

Well, if you've noticed some areas that need changing in your church, then your pastor, if they are doing their job well, has also noticed these things. And it's altogether possible that they don't really know where to start either. Maybe if just one person was to meet with them and talk about it, they could figure it out together.

Maybe they could get a plan started, or, at least, they wouldn't think they were the only ones. Or perhaps, your energy, drive, and excitement can inspire them to get something started.

Or better yet, just do it.

Maybe you go to a big church like I do, where the plan is pretty much in place, and things are being done, and there isn't really a suggestion box so to speak. Or perhaps the leadership of your church isn't as driven as they used to be. It's possible that the top-down model isn't easily accessible for you. Change doesn't have to start from the top.

We can start small.

Your church probably has small group settings of some kind. They may call it Sunday school, or community groups, or life groups, or maybe you just have a group of friends at your church. Perhaps you don't need to start with your whole church, maybe you need to start with your group. Your "church".

The answer is going to be different for each situation. But it's always going to start with individuals. Probably just one. Maybe you?

I think we all want our churches to be places where people are celebrating. We want our churches to be known for helping their communities. We want people to notice our churches. I would love for your church's honest sign to say exactly what you want it to say. And if it doesn't right now, maybe the change needs to start with you.

Drive over to your church. Kick down the sign out front. Rename it. And then live up to the name.

Make Carl proud.

The Easy Part

"Do The Easy Part" Was The Original Title Of This Book. But It's A Way Better Chapter Title. Don't You Think?

This book originally had a different title and a very long subtitle.

Do The Easy Part

How to live out your faith when you don't feel qualified, don't know the answers, and don't feel like it.

Catchy.

These are three huge barriers to expressing our faith through love. Big enough to warrant a subtitle. But the book went through some re-branding; so now, it's a chapter instead of a full-length book. (You're welcome).

As far as I can tell, these are the three huge ideas holding people back from living out their faith. There are plenty of other excuses as well I'm sure, but it seems to me most of us find ourselves fitting into one of these categories.

For some of us, we just don't feel qualified.

Maybe we grew up in church, but we haven't been in a long time. Maybe we just started going. Maybe we have that one thing that we just can't seem to shake. Maybe if we admit it, we've been Sunday Christians this whole time. (You know, go to church on Sunday, and live like hell all week. These are the kind of Christian clichés I grew up with). Maybe we curse, or drink, or have a temper. Or maybe we have a rough past, and we really just don't think we can be used anymore. Maybe we think we're broken. Worthless. For whatever reason, big or small, we feel unqualified.

Then there is a group of us that don't feel like we know the answers.

When it comes down to it, there are some pretty tricky questions in Christianity. Some of us feel like we can't share what we believe or can't live out our faith, or can't participate in something because we don't know the right answers. Some of us have only just mastered the basics. Some of us realized as soon as we figured out an answer, it just lead to more questions. Some of us are nervous that we'll misrepresent Jesus, say the wrong thing, chase someone away, or worse.

What if they ask me about homosexuality? What if they want to talk about alcohol? What if some other hot button issue comes up, and we disagree, and I don't know how to "Defend my faith"? Or how am I supposed to say I'm a Christian when I don't even know anything about atonement theories? Or how to spell transubstantiation? And I don't have much Scripture memorized. And what if I don't know the answer?

And then there's this last one. We don't feel like it.

(This is my world. If you resonate with this one, understand you're in good company. We're really fun people, and you'll fit right in). Maybe it's not so much that we don't know what to do, or don't feel like we're the ones to do it. Maybe, if we're honest, we just don't want to. We don't! Maybe we're just too tired. Maybe it just sounds like too much work to volunteer, go to a meeting, or lead a small group. Maybe we feel like going to church is enough, we really shouldn't be asked to do more than that, and we just don't want to. Maybe when it comes down to it, we can't name why, we just don't want to.

Or maybe it's just with specific people that we have a really hard time being Jesus. There's that co-worker who is conniving and manipulative but still gets the promotion. And then there's the guy doing five under in the passing lane and thinking everything is just fine. Maybe it's a family member who you know didn't actually change and you're not going to be the one caught off guard. Or the person in the grocery store that rams your Achilles tendon with their shopping cart. Maybe it's the person in the pew behind you that you know is going to start gossiping the moment the last song is over. We don't feel like it because they don't deserve more Jesus in our eyes.

There are a thousand reasons not to live out our faith; to not be Jesus in this world. Some of them are better than others, but none of them are good enough. (This book assumes that you think there should be more Jesus in the world). Sometimes it's really hard. It just is. However, I think in all of these situations, there is a simple solution.

Do the easy part.

Do the easy part? What on earth do you mean by this?

I'm glad you asked.

Do The Easy Part

In its simplest form, doing the easy part means taking the first step toward living out your faith. It means finding the easiest part of the thing you think you should do and doing that first. It means starting small, but it means starting. It means looking at the place you think you should be, qualified, informed, desiring, whatever it is, and moving in that direction.

Let's look at a few examples of how this can work.

Yeah, I'm Not Your Guy

Let's suppose you find yourself in the *I don't feel qualified* category. You think you should be doing more, and you would like to do more, but you don't think you're the person for the job. Great! Start with the easy part.

Let's imagine you've only been going to church for a few months. You want to get started volunteering, but really don't feel qualified to lead a small group, pray out loud, or anything really. But you notice that your church puts out coffee on Sunday mornings, or they do on most Sundays. Sometimes it's there, sometimes it's empty, and sometimes it's nowhere to be found. That's easy enough, you love coffee, and serve it to people all the time! So, you decide to start being the person that fills the coffee pots on Sunday morning.

That's where you start. Everybody feels qualified to serve coffee.

The point is, you start! In a moment we've gone from not feeling qualified to express our faith, to serving people on a weekly basis. The point is not if we do something big or life-changing for people. The point is we start. We start small. We're faithful in little things, and then who knows what opportunities it can lead to?

Say What Now?

Now, what about those of us who feel like we don't know the answers? Maybe we feel like we don't know enough to represent Jesus. Maybe we've never really read the Bible or we've only heard a few stories, or maybe we keep changing our mind about what we think about things! How are we supposed to introduce people to Jesus? How can we defend our faith? How will we know what to do?

I'll say it again. Do the easy part.

There are some parts of Christianity that are complicated. (There, I said it). Some parts are trickier than others, some questions don't have clear answers, and some parts have multiple answers that we will never completely agree on. Luckily, we have plenty of time to figure those parts out. We don't need to know *all* of the answers to know *some* of the answers.

For example, check out this section from 1 John

> *If someone has enough money to live well and sees a brother or sister in need but shows no compassion—how can God's love be in that person? Dear children, let's not merely say that we love each other; let us show the truth by our actions.*

You don't need a degree to understand that one. If we see someone in need, we have to help! Feed the hungry! Shelter the homeless! These are not complicated ideas! You don't need to do any research, consult any thought leaders, read any blogs, or get a second opinion to act on this one. Maybe you have questions about other parts, but this part is clear. Well then, do it!

Start with what's clear, start with the easy part! The Bible is just full of statements that are easy to understand. And if those other questions come up, look up the answers along the way, or just don't worry about them. Just keep doing the part you understand.

Nope, Don't Like That

Or what if we don't feel like it. Maybe you're like me, and it's actually pretty easy to represent Jesus to some people. And for others…nothing has ever been harder. Pick your person; the bad driver, the rude co-worker, the nagging mother-in-law… maybe it's a lot of people, maybe just the one. Either way, you may just not be ready to invite them over for Sunday lunch. Maybe you can't stand the idea of getting coffee with them, and helping them move sounds like a punishment fit for war criminals. Fine, don't start there. Start with the easy part.

Maybe you decide you're going to send them a text, not a call, one morning this week, saying the nicest thing you can think to say to them. Maybe you decide to pray for them. Maybe you're not even there yet, and you need to just try and come up with one redeeming quality about them. Perhaps you should sit next to them at church once.

If it's a relationship that you want to salvage, start small. Don't try to be best friends, that's not your job. Your job is to be Jesus, as best you can, in their life. So, start with the easy part, and who knows? Maybe you get that coffee together someday.

Getting Started

Here's the thing about the easy part; sometimes, the easy part is actually easy to do, like filling coffee pots. But other times, the easy part just means we know what we should do, like volunteering our time, feeding the hungry, and loving our enemies. Sometimes, in order to do the easy part, we still have to step out of our comfort zone.

But that's okay! Everything great happens when we're at least a little uncomfortable! We need more people that are uncomfortable. We need more people starting with the easy part.

The truth is, we don't need everyone to do the hard part. But we do need everyone to do the easy part. It's ok to not be ready for the hardest parts right now. It's ok to start with the easy part. But we do need everyone to start.

We need more Jesus in this world! Even if it's just the easy part. We really can't get enough, but for some reason we get caught up in these excuses.

I'm not qualified

I don't know the answers

I don't feel like it

I...fill in the blank

It's like we get caught up in the idea that we have to do all or nothing. Like there's no middle ground between being a saint and a heathen. Like if we're not going to start a non-profit, there's no point. And if we're not going to be a pastor, then why try. Or if we don't feel like we can lead a small group right now, there's nothing for us to do. Like we can't get started if we haven't passed the test.

For some reason, we get caught up in thinking that doing a little is worse than doing nothing.

What I love about the easy part is, God does not look for people in the right place. He looks for people *moving in the right direction*. God doesn't say, "I want you to get here before I can use you."

He just says, "I want you to come this way." I want you to come toward *me*. I want you to *start*. God doesn't always give us a destination to get to, but he gives us a direction. The easy part means moving in that direction and taking that first step.

Start with one minute

Start with one verse

One Sunday

One phone call

One time

We don't have to worry about the hard part right now. We just need to get started.

I absolutely do not believe that God will be disappointed in us for taking a small step. I do not believe God is frustrated that you're not doing more. I don't think God cares that you're not burning yourself out, or that you're hesitant, or even afraid.

If you pray for one minute, God doesn't ask why you didn't do five. He just loves the minute! If you volunteer once he doesn't ask why you don't lead the group; he's just glad you volunteered once. This is not an all or nothing deal. We can take small steps in the right direction.

When Jesus is asked what the greatest commandment is, he says "Love God." And then he follows up with, "Love People."

Love God. Love People.

That's not hard to understand. There are no qualifications to do that. And we all want to be loved. At some place, perhaps deep inside of us, we want to love people too. We know we should. Sometimes, we overcomplicate things by over thinking, or dwelling on something we're hung up on, or letting anger, fear, jealousy or some other emotion get in the way. But at the end of the day, loving God, and loving people has some pretty simple first steps we can all take.

So, what's your next step? What's the easiest thing you can think of to move you in the right direction? What does the easy part look like for you? Don't wait. I know it's a little uncomfortable. But we need you. We need more people trying to look more like Jesus. Take the first step. What is the very easiest first step you can think of? Find that step and take it. Start with the easy part.

My Little Girl

I think you learn a lot about God when you have a baby. I would assume any parent would tell you this, but it wasn't obvious to me until I had one of my own. I've thought of three quick lessons that my daughter, Colbie, taught me in the first year of her life, and I'd like to share them with you.

I know you're crying

When my daughter was only a few months old, we tried to let her do something called self-soothing. Self-soothing is exactly what it sounds like; when the baby gets upset and begins crying, you don't rush to them and pick them up, you let them cry for a little while and settle down on their own. Sounds great in theory. Sounds loud, and frantic, and terrible in reality.

We didn't last long.

But one day, I was home alone with her, and she started crying in her crib. So, I decided to let her try to self-soothe, but I did go into the room with her. She's crying in her crib, and I'm probably on Twitter on my phone in the chair next to her. What's interesting in this situation is how little she understands.

In her world, tragedy has struck. She woke up, in a room alone, her diaper was wet, she was probably frightened; she was always confused (I cannot imagine how confusing life must be for a baby) and she was upset. She is frustrated and starts to whine. But as she realizes nobody is coming to help, she starts screaming, crying, and just freaking out. (By the way, she was one of the loudest babies ever. That's not me saying that; the nurses in the hospital, who see lots of babies, told us that. And we agreed).

From her perspective, the world is basically ending, and nobody has any idea. What she doesn't know is that I'm sitting three feet from her. She doesn't know that I specifically came into the room to make sure she was okay before letting her try to work it out herself. She didn't know that I knew that everything was going to be fine. She didn't know that I knew, or that I was there.

And I couldn't help but think that maybe that's how God feels with us. We have such a small perspective. Sometimes, we can only see what's going on right in front of us. Sometimes, we don't like what's happening, and we wonder if God can really see us. We wonder if he hears us. Sometimes, what's happening really is bad, it really does suck, and it really hurts us. And in those moments, it makes so much sense to yell, and scream, and curse. It's so natural to yell, "Why aren't you helping me!? Don't you hear me!?"

It's really easy to forget that God never leaves us. He always comes in to check on us and make sure we're okay. He always knows. And just like my little girl couldn't possibly understand why I didn't pick her up right away, we don't always understand God's timing, purpose, or plan. But that doesn't mean He's not watching. It doesn't mean He doesn't know, and it doesn't mean He's not sitting next to us with it.

I just want to hold you

Colbes had a rough week a little while ago where she was waking up in the middle of the night. She rarely does this, so for her to do it several nights in a row was rough to adjust to again. Everyone in the house was just kind of tired for the week.

Fun fact about our daughter; she does not like to be held. She is squirmy and will get frustrated really quickly if not allowed to walk around on her own. She literally yells, "Free, Free!" when she wants to be put down and let free.

So, one of these tired mornings, I hear her wake up. But I'm tired, and I don't really want to follow her around the living room. I love playing games with her and letting her be free, but this morning, I felt more like just holding her. I would rather cuddle together and read a book or two before really getting into the day. So, instead of bringing her out to the living room with the toys, I went back to her nursery, left the lights low, picked her up, and rocked her in our rocking chair.

Without the extra stimulation, the light, the toys, the routine of it all, she settled down with me and just relaxed, and cuddled in. She was content, and I was overjoyed. I don't get a lot of cuddle time with her anymore, and it was a really simple, yet special moment for both of us. We sat there for about half an hour just enjoying the time together before going out to the toys, games, and food that the day had for us.

I think sometimes we forget how much Jesus loves spending time with us—just spending time with us. I know I get caught up in *doing* all the time. *I need to do this, and this and this, so that I can do*...I love to keep busy. But I think a lot of us forget that we don't have to keep busy all the time.

We have a tendency to measure our relationship with Jesus by how much we've done for him and with him. We need to volunteer more at church, or we need to plan more events or feed more people. And these are good things, but they don't replace just spending time with him. We don't look at other relationships in our life like this. But we do it with Jesus all the time.

Throughout the Bible, Jesus is constantly stopping and just spending time with God. And he didn't have a devotional, or a guitar, or even a Bible. He was just spending time with God. He wasn't always doing. Sometimes, Jesus just wants to hold us. Sometimes, we don't need to do; we need to just be.

I love you buddy

I remember the day she was born like it was yesterday. Well, I guess I remember moments like they were yesterday, honestly the whole day is kind of a blur. But I remember the first time we saw her. And I remember the first time I held her. My wife was being helped with some kind of procedure, and a nurse, rather unceremoniously, handed me this little, pink swaddled bundle—my little girl.

I had known her name for months, but we had never met. I already knew I loved her, what I didn't know was how much.

(Which is like the cheesiest, most clichéd thing a person can say, but stick with me). I remember feeling two things. The first was the overwhelming love I expected, and everyone expects from holding their new child. What I didn't expect was the other feeling. I didn't expect the deep, primal, protective instinct I immediately felt. It was a wild, frightening feeling. I understood just how far I would go to protect her, and how there was no limit to what I would do.

I would die for her.

If you had asked me 24 hours before that moment if I had ever loved someone, I would have said yes. Of course I have! I'm married to my incredible wife! And it wasn't that I didn't love her, it was just that I didn't know how capable of love I was. I didn't know there was another entire level that I had never felt before. I thought I had loved. I thought I had cared and been downright passionate. But I didn't know there was more.

What's amazing is, even at our very best, we cannot understand God's love. Even as we continue to discover just how capable of loving each other we are, we only start to scratch the surface. We can't know or understand a perfect love. And yet, it's offered to us.

I imagine this is how God looks at us every time. I imagine the only thing he can manage to say when he sees us is, "I love you buddy." The same thing I said to my daughter the day we met. There's no time for being disappointed, or frustrated with us. There's no condemnation for someone you love that much. There's no time for anything but, "Wow. I love him. I would die for her." And I know that, because He did.

God's love is perfect, but I imagine it just keeps growing for us anyway. That's easy to forget sometimes because our imperfect love is conditional. There have been a few times already that I've raised my voice at my daughter. I've been frustrated with her and even been angry with her. Even our greatest understanding of love doesn't come close to what Jesus feels toward us. But I think I got a small glimpse of it that evening in the hospital.

Those Stupid People Are People

Let's Get Down To Business. Church Business.

I've only sat through a few church business meetings in my life. You know, where all of the church members sit in the sanctuary, there's a guy with a mic that we all know but have to refer to as the moderator for a while, and big decisions are made for the church by the church.

I hate these meetings.

But I do remember one in particular. It was a hot day, and this particular meeting lasted close to three hours. (Seriously, just shoot me in the head). What I remember most about this meeting was that we spent an hour discussing whether or not the church should accept free playground equipment. Yes, you heard that right—an *hour* discussing *free* stuff.

What was most interesting was how quickly the discussion dissolved. Before long, there were two sides that disagreed. Shortly after, there was a passive aggressive comment, followed by outright finger pointing, and ending with one individual standing up and saying, *I can't help but think…if Jesus were here…who would he agree with?*

Then we voted to accept the equipment, 97% for, 2% against, 1% abstaining. And that is why I no longer attend business meetings.

I want to talk about important conversations in this chapter, and I've used the example above in an attempt to avoid discussing politics, though the political landscape and the discussions that surround it are actually better examples.

I'd like to discuss hard conversations because if there is a group of people that needs to be able to articulate a thought without getting flustered, leaching onto a bigger group, or my goodness calling someone stupid, it should be Christians. I would love for that to be the thing we're known for because people would listen, and what we have to say, needs to be heard.

I have two primary concerns with the way important conversation are going that I would like to address:

1. There are no groups to be a part of. There is no *us*. There is no *them*.

2. We really need to stop calling each other stupid.

Us Vs. Them

Let's start by addressing the "Us Vs. Them" mentality. Very simply I think we need to let go of the idea that there is an "us" that we agree with and a "them" that we disagree with. Primarily because this is simply not true.

Pick a group, any group, pick one that you associate with—Democrats, Chargers fans, Baptists, moms against _____, any group at all. It's really easy to fall into the idea that we just agree with these groups. But the truth is, these groups are made of individuals. They're made of individual people with a wide range of ideas, thoughts, and beliefs. And not even two of them completely agree on everything. Not a chance.

Have you ever in your life met someone that you agree with completely? Maybe you told them you did, but did you? I haven't. We may agree on a few things, but not on everything. Certainly, not on something as broad as politics or religion.

And that's just one person! How could we think there is an "Us" out there that completely agrees with us? Sure, we agree on a few issues, but the idea of saying *I'm a part of a group and I completely agree with this group*, is just silly.

This is especially dangerous in church. We have people that decide what they believe based on what their church or denomination says. Some denominations even get together to change their belief statements and expect people to just follow along. We cannot have people claiming to follow Christ who don't have their own beliefs. What we believe is far too important to leave to others to decide for us.

So no, we don't agree with everything our pastors say. We don't agree with everything Baptists say. We don't agree with everything Rob Bell says, or Annie Downs, or Beth Moore

(GASP!). There is no "Us" to be a part of. We're all people with our own thoughts that disagree with everyone at some place or another. And that's ok. It's even good.

(Quick side note here. When we disagree with someone in a matter of faith, it is important that we recognize that we disagree in one area, and not in every area. The word *heretic* is used far too often in religious discussion and debate. We disqualify or discredit someone based on one thing they think, when the odds are very good that we've disagreed with them in the past, and we will disagree with them again in the future. If we disagree with someone on one issue, we don't have to throw out everything they've ever said. If we don't like one book, we don't have to burn the rest. If we don't like a tweet, we don't have to unfollow them. And one statement cannot undo their (or my) theology. Seriously guys, let's just relax here).

So, not only is it not even a real option, it is dangerous.

If we believe that we are making decisions with a group of "Us," then it becomes very easy to assume the same of other people. If we believe we can be part of "Us," we then believe others must be part of "Them." We reduce people into groups, assume we know everything they have to say, and label them as *other*, or even worse, *wrong*.

And once we know what group to file someone into, and we've decided we know exactly what they are going to say, the conversation is dead. There is no talking, no brainstorming, and no discussion. We stop trying to solve the problem. There is nothing left to do but start name-calling, because we can't even find a starting point to talk to each other anymore.

Brené Brown discusses this issue at length in her book, "Braving the Wilderness". (Seriously, go buy everything she has ever written. She's so much smarter than me). In it she writes:

> The only true option is to refuse to accept the terms of the argument by challenging the framing of the debate. But make no mistake; this is opting for the wilderness. Why? Because the argument is set up to silence dissent and draw lines in the sand that squelch debate, discussion, and questions—the very processes that we know lead to effective problem solving… When we engage in the "us versus them" argument, we lose. The only person who wins is the person who owns the framing of the argument.

The solution to the "Us vs. Them" mentality is simple; we refuse to take part in it. When people are taking sides, we do the unbearably brave thing and stand in the middle. We refuse to listen to groups and instead talk to individuals. We don't let ourselves be defined by a group, no matter how closely they resemble our opinions. We simply don't do it. We see people for what they are, individuals who we may agree or disagree with.

This might mean answering questions in strange ways.

Are you a Republican? No. I'm Andy. I have political views, but they are complex and multi-layered, and they don't fit into one category or another.

Are you a Baptist? No. I'm Andy. I have strong beliefs about Jesus, but I don't think they line up with any one denomination.

Are you one of those gun control people? I don't know. I'm Andy. I have opinions about that, but they don't really fit into the box you're suggesting.

It's going to feel strange for sure, but it's well worth it if we can avoid us vs. them arguments, and have important conversations that need to be had.

And now, on to a, perhaps less important, but more annoying conversation.

They Are Not Stupid

For the love of Jen Hatmaker, can we stop calling each other stupid? Every time I see an important discussion start on social media, it ends the same way.

Your Stupid! (I used the wrong "you're" on purpose by the way).

Seriously? Name-calling? A group of adults lining up across from another group of adults and calling each other stupid? "Us vs. "Them" will bring a conversation to a halt, but the name-calling is even worse. It actually changes the conversation. We start with an important issue that both sides feel needs addressed. But name-calling changes that conversation into a debate about which side is smarter. Do you see the problem here?

We've become more interested in who's smarter, and more importantly, why the other side is stupid. And when we do this,

We don't solve the issue!

If our point is to prove that people who disagree with us are stupid; WE DO NOT HAVE A POINT. We no longer need to say what we're saying; it doesn't matter. We're not being helpful, and we're not trying to solve the problem. *You're super smart, fine, just go away while we fix the problem.*

Can we get to a point where we recognize that there are people smarter than us, with better points than us, with more education, more statistics and more experience than us *on both sides*? I know for a fact that *none* of my friends on social media are political experts in any way. And yet, many times, they feel completely comfortable calling an entire political party and their supporters, idiots. That's actually pretty impressive. (I suppose there would be some irony in my calling them stupid for this behavior. We'll stick with impressive).

(By the way, I never see Jesus call anyone stupid. He's mean to some people for sure, and I like to imagine him as really sarcastic. But I never see him cutting off the conversation to prove how smart he is.)

They are not stupid. We just don't like the way they want to solve the problem. We just disagree. You can disagree with smart people. (And if you disagree with that, then you disagree with me. And I'm like, super smart).

We cannot allow important conversations to be reduced to trying to prove who's smarter. Important conversations aren't about winning arguments; they're about addressing issues, solving problems, brainstorming, disagreeing in a civil way and working toward a solution. A conversation can never be reduced to *you're stupid* for any reason. It's a terrible habit that we've seen climb all the way to presidential debates. And if it's not going to happen in important conversations, it can't happen in day-to-day conversations.

I think what is most frustrating for me about this subject is just how much time we're wasting. There are real problems that need to be discussed, and not just on a political and social level, but on an individual level. We should be able to have hard conversations with our friends, our spouses, and even our in-laws without getting frustrated.

We may not have the influence to affect the powers that be on our own, but we do need to be influencing those in our circle. We need to be having these conversations on a micro level because we need to impact our community. We need to impact our homes. And if we can't have important conversations on that level, then we risk not solving important issues.

This applies to so much more than guns and other political issues. Yes, it's important for gun control, and abortion, and immigration, and refugees, and war, and healthcare and a huge number of big complicated concepts that most of us only grasp in part. But it's also super important for how we speak to our neighbors, co-workers, friends, and people behind us at church. It matters for small conversations like when to get married, what car to buy, how much to save, Coke or Pepsi, best football teams, least heretical preachers, and even for if you like Starbucks more than Dunkin. Because if it's going to stop in the big conversations, it can't exist in the small conversations either.

If we can't talk about it, we can't work together to fix it. I'm going to say this a thousand times if I have to. *We both agree that something needs to change.* We can't let our differences in opinion distract us from focusing on the issue at hand. Isn't it ironic that in trying to defend the best way to solve a serious problem, we get distracted from solving that problem?

Can we start from, and stay in a place where we both remember that we want something to change? I want to do it this way, and you want to do it that way, but it does need to change.

Some Simple Suggestions

I think several things need to happen in order for these important conversations to happen.

First, we need to have these conversations with people we are invested in, not with people we only know from their social profiles; people we actually know, love, and trust. People we care about, and whose opinions have the power to shape ours. We tend to have important conversations with just whoever happens to be willing to talk about it. Often because we took the bait, and are now listening to a one-sided conversation from someone we don't even recognize.

But when we speak to people we are invested in; their words become more powerful. They are not only facts and figures, but also opinions that we are interested in. Suddenly, something doesn't have to be empirically accurate to hold weight. What they say matters, because of who is saying it.

Second, I think these conversations need to happen in person. There's something about being online, in a comment section, text message, email, or YouTube comment that brings out the worst in us. Perhaps it's the perceived anonymity; maybe it's just easy to do because we don't truly see the result of our words. They just sit there until the calculated response of whoever we've addressed finally pops up. (It's so easy to lie and say something doesn't bother you online).

What's interesting is, I've never met a person who talks the way some people do online in person. I've never met a person who will just throw themselves into stranger's conversations and proceed to insult them to their face. I rarely see people cite sources in person; I see much less vulgarity, and truly, I've never seen someone threaten someone's family in person because they disagree on something.

Important conversations need to happen with people we care about, and they need to happen in person. We have to be able to have small conversations if we ever hope to have bigger, more important conversations. Christ followers need to be the people who can have important conversations without it dissolving into nothing, because the conversation we want to have, is *really* important.

So, let's recap briefly.

There is no us.

There is no them.

There are people. We agree with all of them on some points. We disagree with all of them on other points.

We need to stop calling each other stupid.

We need to have conversations with people we care about, and in person.

Because if we don't, we'll never solve any of the important issues that need solving.

And if you don't agree with me,

You're stupid.

(Please tell me you read that with the right tone. It's really funny).

Cheers

Can We Just…

Look, I'll just say it.

I drink. (GASP!)

I like beer the most, I think wine is fine, and I really enjoy a good whiskey. I could spend a chapter trying to convince you that it's ok to drink, and explain why I think so (I'll give you a hint; it deals with Jesus turning water into something else) but you've probably heard that conversation before. Plus, I think it would be wasted, as I think you probably agree with me on this anyway. Besides, I'd much rather laugh at Christians' relationship with alcohol than try to defend my stance. For example…

I Just Love The Olives Here

Have you ever run into someone you know from church at the liquor store? Mary mother of awkward. It's an amazing experience.

In many places, you can buy alcoholic beverages right in the grocery store. This is good because it gives you options. For example, if you happen to have a bottle of wine and a twelve pack of PBR in your cart, and see a friend from church, you can just abandon ship.

Oh, Hi Sheryl! Good heavens to Betsy look! Some degenerate has left a shopping cart full of alcohols right next to me! I'm just here for cream cheese; well it was nice seeing you Sheryl!

Here, we can just run away and circle back to get our cart in a few minutes. This is a nice option when it is an option. I, however, live in Pennsylvania, where we like to segregate our foods and alcohols into food stores, beer stores, and wine-and-liquor stores (Why?).

So should you happen to run into a friend in a wine-and-liquor store; things become much more complicated. We have to do a little dance that looks like this:

Did they see me? I don't think they saw me. Should I try to hide behind something? No, then you'll look like a drunk and a crazy person if they find you. Should I just say hi? Oh crap, they definitely just saw me, "Sheryl! Hi! You know I didn't even realize they sold alcohol (whispered) *here. I'm just here for the olives; well it was so great seeing you Sheryl!"*

Yeah, not going to work.

Your only hope at this point is that you're holding a bottle of red wine (because you know, antioxidants) and not a handle of Captain Morgan. Because good luck trying to talk your way out of that one. *Yeah, my dog suffers from night blindness, and the alcohol is the only thing that helps. It's not for me...*

Double Date Double Shot

Or what about the first time you go on a double date with church friends? Is there anything worse in the world than a dry double date? (Yes. There are so many things that are worse. Just let me be dramatic!)

We've never been out with these friends before, and we haven't had "The Talk" with them, so now we both have to do the first double date drink dance. It starts with waiting to see what they order to drink. But naturally, the waiter person asks you what you'll have first, so we decide to just get a water *for now*.

The dance continues throughout the meal as we casually mention the alcohol specials like it's just something we happened to notice and found interesting.

Oh, two for one Bud Lights... I see they have beer specials going on, that seems like a good deal... Oh, there's a bar over there, how interesting...

This doesn't seem to be working, so we decide we're just going to go for it and order a drink. So now, we try to gauge just what we can pull off here. Should we go for a glass of red wine, is beer a safer option, or are these full on margarita friends?

When we finally figure that out, we now try to signal to our significant other that we're going to order something to drink, and when we do we would like for them not to make us drink alone in case our new friends don't order anything.

And then the waiter comes back, and we decide not to go for it.

And we wish we had, and so does your spouse, and you can see the friends you're with are dancing the exact same dance, and finally, one of you just kind of blurts out in the middle of conversation, "*DoYouGuysDrink?!*" At which point everyone exhales, has a short laugh, and can just talk openly about it.

And the dance is done.

I feel like I should clarify here, that I'm not one of those obsessed with alcohol people, but you know the tension of not knowing is real, and that a pitcher of margaritas is the perfect conversation lubricant for a first double date.

Grandma's Coming To Town

Or don't we all have the one relative that thinks it's wrong? So, we have to hide all of the drinks and drinking paraphernalia when they come over. (Why don't we just go to their house?)

But we have to go through the whole checklist. *Did I get the beers out of the bottom drawer in the fridge? What about the liquor cabinet, did you empty that out? What about the wine glasses, do we have to hide stemware? Why else would we have it? Kids, it's okay to lie to grandma about just this one thing.*

It's always fun when grandma visits. Hopefully, she never figures out why you keep going down to the garage for like ten minutes and then brushing your teeth.

The Most Sound Biblical Argument For Alcohol You Will Ever Read

But alcohol can bring people together too. Honestly, I think there's a reason Jesus turned water into wine for his first miracle.

I think a few of the disciples were on the fence about him. Thomas was doubtful in particular. (Poor Thomas. What a bummer of a legacy to leave. Honestly, I would have done exactly the same thing...But I'm still going to make jokes at his expense). I think some of the disciples were wondering if this was really what they wanted to do with their life. And then Jesus was like, *Hey guys. Check this out.*

The disciples see Jesus turn water into wine, run over, and just line right up behind him like, *We never doubted you for a moment!* To which Jesus probably rolled his eyes and moved on.

But if you couple this party trick with another well-known miracle involving fish and loaves and the multiplication of food? These guys had a pretty good thing going. I imagine them going out to eat, and Peter just ordering for the table.

"Yes, we'll have one steak, one lobster tail, and twelve *waters*" As he winks at the other disciples. Jesus would have thrown the best Super Bowl parties.

And that my friends, is what is known as sound, biblical, exegesis.

Relax. Unwind. Uncork

Honestly, I wish more Christ followers and churches would be openly okay with alcohol. (Not saying you should be. Just that if you are, you shouldn't feel the need to hide it). The vast majority of Christians I know are fine with it and even enjoy it, yet many still feel tension and shame around the subject. I wish we didn't do this to ourselves.

I think small groups should be fine with having drinks together. I absolutely think we can discuss Jesus over a Cabernet, and people feel more comfortable sharing with each other during a round of Sam Adam's. It brings people together. It adds a level of familiarity and comfort to a conversation. And without question, I think men's groups should start with tequila shots. Not joking. You want men to talk? Let them have a drink.

For some reason, many of us are still making a big deal about something I think we can move on from. I would love it if we could stop doing these social dances around alcohol and just enjoy a drink together shame free.

But I'm not going to be the one to tell Grandma.

Cheers!

Your One Thing

I Will Look For You. I Will Find You. And I Will Kill You.

When I was in college, a movie came out called *Taken*. *Taken* is a movie starring Liam Neeson about a man trying to save his abducted daughter before she is sold into slavery. The movie itself is pretty great; it involves a lot of hand-to-hand combat, car chases, and of course, threatening people over the phone. While I enjoyed the movie, it started a conversation around human trafficking that I enjoyed much less. Suddenly, on our little Christian college campus, there were talks, and videos, and panels, and lectures that we could attend all centered on human trafficking. And at first, I went to all of them.

I remember going to these talks and afterward thinking, *we have to do something about this.* And then I would go to another talk and think, *something needs to be done about this.*

And then I'd go to another and think, *We really have to do something about this.* And that became the pattern.

Go to seminar.

Get pumped up.

Think something should be done.

Repeat.

Do you maybe see a problem with this pattern? Perhaps the part where I never actually do anything? Yeah, I noticed it too. So, eventually, I just stopped going to the talks. Eventually, I became frustrated with myself for not doing anything, and I didn't want to walk away from another seminar feeling guilty. Instead of hearing more, I just quit all together.

This wasn't the only issue I was introduced to in college. I went to talks about people in Haiti affected by an earthquake, refugees from various countries, women's rights activists, people fighting for orphans, individuals who volunteer with the homeless, LGBT rights…all of it. I heard about all of it, really thought I should do something, and then went to another seminar.

It occurred to me that I had become what I now call a *passive activist*.

A passive activist is exactly what it sounds like. It's someone who knows a problem exists, feels passionately that something should be done, will even go so far as to tell other people about the problem, but then does nothing to solve the problem. They don't actually engage. It's exactly what I was doing in school.

Passive activism is troublesome for several reasons, and it has reached epidemic proportions. Luckily, I think there's a pretty simple solution. But first, let's look into what we're talking about a little more.

Overload

If you've spent any time on social media lately, you know that there are hundreds of causes that all want our attention. There are hundreds and thousands of needs that all need to be met and the internet has made it possible for us to know about all of them. This is a good thing, but it can also be overwhelming.

Do you ever just kind of feel like you've gotten accustomed to seeing tragedy? Do you see videos about people that need help and just kind of shrug your shoulders? *Oh, great, another thing that's gone wrong.*

Sometimes, I feel like our exposure to all of these needs causes us to feel overwhelmed. Doesn't it just seem like there's nothing to do when we get hit with wave after wave of posts, videos, petitions, fundraisers…?

Please help our veterans

Please help our refugees

Please help our patients

Please help these animals

Please help this disaster relief effort

Please help…

Don't you just feel like throwing your hands up and yelling? *Well, the world is screwed, and there's nothing to do about it!*

There's just too much to do. How could we possibly make a difference? Not only are there too many needs to keep track of, but the issues themselves are huge! How am I supposed to honestly feel like I'm making a difference in issues like systemic racism, homelessness, or cancer when I'm just one person?

It can feel overwhelming, and honestly, hopeless at times.

Fortunately, I think there's a simple answer. (That requires a lot of hard work).

Your OneThing

I think the solution to this problem is fairly simple.

Pick one thing.

I told you it was simple. Pick one thing, and fix it. Pick one thing, and become an expert. Pick one thing and stick with it. Pick one thing and work it until it's done. Pick one thing… and solve it. *This seems too simple to work. There's too much to do; I can't pick just one, what about this!? And what if I pick the wrong one!? And what if I pick this and then that doesn't get done!?*

I know.

Slow down, let me explain. The simplicity of this actually works in our favor, because if we all fix one thing, then everything gets fixed. It's pretty simple math. There are a lot of issues in the world, but there are more people. If we are all committed to solving at least one issue to its completion, then we don't have to worry about other issues not being fixed, because we know we are doing our part. (Not to mention that if we are fixing one thing, it could benefit in the fixing of something else).

The "One Thing" isn't necessarily a hard rule. I suppose someone could handle two, maybe even three issues that they're passionate about. The point is to focus. The point is to really narrow down and set a goal. The point is to find the area that we are really willing to put time, money, and effort into. We need to find an issue where we are willing to go one inch wide, and one mile deep.

We do this by looking at what we're passionate about. What is the thing that you can't stop thinking about? What makes you angry? What keeps you up at night? What is the conversation that you can't get out of your head? Which viral video genuinely inspired you? What's the thing that you feel guilty about not helping? What is it that you would be willing to dedicate your life to? What issue do you look at and say *solving that could be my legacy.*

And then we dive in! It may start by just giving some money. It may start by donating some time. Maybe there's even a brief research portion, but once we've picked our thing, we get busy. It's not one of the things that we share on social media once. We dive in. We start. We ignore that voice in our head that says we can't, or we don't feel like it, because we have to fix this thing. We can't stand for it for another minute. When we think we can't; we do it anyway. When we don't feel qualified, we get qualified.

Thanks For Sharing

We should probably take a minute to talk about raising awareness. (I'd like to raise awareness about raising awareness).

Raising awareness is a good thing, and it has its place, but it has drastically overstepped what it was intended to be. What we've run into today is people, and I've definitely been a part of these people, who never get past raising awareness in the issue they care about.

You probably have that one friend who keeps filling your social media page with a different issue every week. (They're usually in their first or second year of college. Not to generalize or anything). They're just walking billboards for every issue in the world, but never pick one and dive in.

I've noticed this trend on social media, the news, and in our conversations. We see an issue, tell people all about it, share videos and tweets and blogs, and then never mention it again when it's not trending anymore. We stand up and yell,

"This is a problem! And this is a problem! And this is a problem!"

We tell people all about it, but we never actually do anything to fix it.

Which is a problem because the people we tell do the same thing we do. They hear about it, and maybe pass it on, but never really think about it. I think we have a setting in our minds that tells us if we hear about something, it's being solved already. *Somebody else will fix that.*

But going viral doesn't solve problems. It just tells people there are problems.

So by all means, tell people about the need. Tell everybody, recruit help, but then give them something to do. Join them. This is our thing. This is the problem we are going to solve. We can't just shout about it; we need boots on the ground.

Wait, But What About...?

One of the really hard parts about this idea is that we're going to have to say no to some things. We're going to have to not get involved in some important issues. There are so many issues that we could dedicate our lives to. There are a lot of things that need solving, and we're just not going to be able to help with all of them. This is one of the greater challenges of living in a world where needs go viral.

I'll be the first one to say that I don't care about stray cats. I just don't care if they live or die. (I know how harsh that sounds. Please, keep reading). I don't want them to suffer, or die, but I'm not going to do anything about it. I'm not. I want somebody to help them, but I'm glad that's somebody else's thing. You have things that you don't care about too. Some things will be easy for us to say no to; others are harder.

Saying no to issues like the opioid crisis, pornography, domestic violence...

Eventually, we're going to have to be willing to say, *That's important. But it's not my thing.*

We can pass these along and know that we are doing our part in fixing the world—in restoring peace. We know that we can't fix every issue, but we're doing our part.

Now, this is not to say that we can't ever do anything else. *Of course not.* When a tragedy occurs, we hit the ground running. When someone is doing a big drive or asking for a donation, by all means, we can help. This isn't to say that we only help certain people. That's not the point. The point is we don't get stuck in feeling like there's too much to do. We don't feel guilt and shame for not solving other problems. We don't let ourselves get sidetracked with helping other issues and forget the one we were working to solve.

We go one inch wide, and one mile deep, in one issue, and we work it until it's done.

Your Thing Is Not More Important

We should probably, also, have a brief conversation about the way we talk about our things as well. Let me say it directly first.

Your one thing is not more important than someone else's.

Even if we think so, even if it objectively is, we don't get to highjack their conversation. We don't get to put them down. If they are doing something to help, we don't get to try and stop them. We don't try to recruit them into our "more important" need.

It's going to be important that we don't compare our things. It's really easy to do, but it doesn't get us anywhere. You've probably seen this happen without really recognizing it. This usually starts with *Yeah, but what about...*

> Somebody mentions stray animals *yeah, but what about homeless people?*
>
> Somebody mentions pain killer addiction, *yeah, but what about the heroin epidemic?*
>
> Somebody mentions obesity, *yeah, but what about cancer?*

It's almost like we try to one-up each other's one thing. And it's easy to do. It's crucial for us to remember that the things that are most important to us don't have to be the most important to other people. If we all fix our one thing, we get everything done. That's actually one of the benefits of having unique perspectives. It means I don't have to help stray cats, and you don't have to work with teenage guys. (Of the two, I'm not sure which is more unruly. Or which smells worse).

My One Thing Is

So, this leads us to the inevitable question.

What is your one thing going to be?

What is it that you are going to be laser-focused on? What are you going to dive into head-first? What's keeping you up at night? What are you just dying to fix? Who do you want to help? What need are you going to meet?

There are so many issues; so many tragedies. And they all need help. If you could help with all of them you would. I know you would. But you can't; you just can't.

So pick one.

Pick one, and dive in.

Pick one, and get qualified.

Pick one, and get obsessed.

Pick one, and fix it.

Pete

One of my favorite characters in the Bible is Peter. What I love so much about Peter is how relatable he is for me. He's just always doing what I feel like I might have done in the situation. He flies off the handle, says dumb stuff, overreacts, makes promises he can't keep, and demands too much of himself. Because of this, he gets kind of a bad rep.

I also get the impression that the other disciples got annoyed with him from time to time, which is why they told so many embarrassing stories about him that we still have today. But I'm glad they included those stories because I think we can learn a lot from Peter. I'm not going to try and cover his whole life here; he did a lot, but I do want to look at a few of my favorite stories from his life mostly because I think they're funny.

Maybe We Could Rollerblade Together Sometime?

Let's revisit for a moment the story of Jesus walking on water. We left off with Jesus walking up to screaming men in a boat and telling them to calm down.

Enter Peter.

He looks out, and sees Jesus walking on the water.

"Hey!" he yells, "Jesus! If that's really you, tell me to come out and walk on the water with you!" (My wording).

Ok, let's start with the part where Peter asks Jesus to clarify that it is, in fact, him out there. Like, who else does he think this is? *Excuse me; I'm pretty sure you are who you say you are, but could I see some identification before I try to stand on this body of water?* I think it's just a really funny thing to do, one that I assume the disciples mocked him for.

But then, we get to the really audacious part of the story. Peter looks out, decides that he is talking to Jesus, and not some Jesus impersonator, and asks to walk on water with Jesus. Now, walking on water is not a common occurrence! This reads the same way that Peter asking Jesus to rollerblade with him would read. But he's asking to walk on water! *Jesus, I do not foresee another opportunity to walk on water, and that looks really neat, so... would it be cool if I just joined you for a minute?*

I always want Jesus to let me do the fun stuff. I want a bigger platform, I want to lead worship, I want to have a successful book, I want to be the funny speaker. Maybe you can relate. I want to do the fun part, and I want to do it when I want to do it.

This really wasn't the time for Peter to walk on water. As you recall, there was a terrible storm going on, and Jesus had a point to make. But Jesus is always so cool. So, when Peter wanted to walk on water, whether it was good timing or not, he got to.

Jesus. Shut-up.

A little while later, Jesus and his twelve friends are walking around. Jesus is doing his thing, and he casually mentions to the disciples that pretty soon, he is going to be arrested, tried, beaten, spit on, dragged out of town and tortured to death by means of crucifixion.

Enter Peter.

Peter takes Jesus aside and yells at him for saying these things, then tells him that it will never happen. Peter's basically like, *Jesus. Shut-up. You're wrong, that'll never happen, stop saying crazy things.* (My wording again).

To which Jesus replies, "Get behind me Satan!" (Not my words. Jesus') Yeah, that's in the Bible. Matthew 16:23 for those of you playing along at home.

Not the best thing to be called by anyone, let alone Jesus! But I think we get to see a side of Peter here that many of us can relate to. Don't you sometimes feel like you have a better plan than God? Doesn't there sometimes seem like there is a better way to get from point A to point B than the way God decided to take us?

Sometimes, I don't like what Jesus has to say. I don't like how Jesus would handle a situation. I don't like asking W.W.J.D. because that's not what I would do! So, I hear you Peter. It would have been nice if Jesus was saying other things. Nicer things. But that's not how it works, and telling Jesus to shut-up is rarely (never) the solution.

That's My Ear Now Sucka!

One of the moments I can relate to most in Peter's life is when Jesus got arrested. The scene looks like this: Jesus and his disciples are in a garden when they see an assembly of torches coming their way. The mob walks up to them, and Jesus takes charge.

"Who are you looking for?"

"We're looking for Jesus."

"Well, that's me. Come and get me." (My wording. Not found in the Bible. But this is how I think it went down).

Jesus has things under control. There's even a part where he speaks and knocks some of the mob down on the ground just with his voice to defend his disciples. He's got this.

Enter Peter.

Out of nowhere, Peter lunges at someone with a sword and cuts his ear off.

As you can imagine, Jesus found this silly, and oh-so, unnecessary. *Dude...we can't take you anywhere. Put the stupid sword away...now I have to fix this guy's ear, like I don't have enough going on right now.* He tells him to put the sword away, heals the guy's ear, and goes back to being Jesus.

I love this story so much. That is exactly what I would do in this situation. Maybe that seems stupid to you, and maybe it is, but try to look at the scene from Peter's point of view. Jesus has been saying weird cryptic things for the last few months about him dying, there's a mob approaching, and this mob is led by one of your boys. One of the guys you've spent the last several years with has decided to kill the guy you've come to call master, teacher, messiah, and friend.

Yeah, I'm not keeping my cool either.

I'm very much a "Ready? Fire! Aim." kind of guy. I like to take action. I like to kick down doors. (Metaphorical doors). If I can't fix something, I'll make sure it's good and broken. I don't like to let Jesus handle situations. I don't like surrendering control. I like action. And I think that's where Peter was at this moment. *I just need to do something.*

But, like always, Jesus had it under control. He always has it under control. So once again, Peter has made a fool of himself and made a mess in the process.

That Guy? Nope. Don't Know That Guy.

We're going to backtrack for just a quick second. Right before Jesus gets arrested, he has dinner with the disciples, commonly called the last supper. And during this dinner, Jesus has something to tell the disciples.

"Ok guys, so you know how I've been predicting my death for a while now? Well, tonight's the night. It's going to get pretty ugly, and all of you are going to bail on me before it's over… No, no, no; it's cool; it's cool. When I'm raised up, we'll all hang out and it'll be fine. But you're all totally going to abandon me." (Again, my wording. This is *my* book, if you want to read the Bible, just go read the Bible).

Enter Peter.

"No way man! I. Will. Never. Abandon. You. Never! Even if everyone else does, I'll be right there. Even if I have to die with you!"

And I just imagine Jesus sighing and smiling at Peter one last time before telling him that he's going to deny knowing him three times in the next 24 hours. *Yeah… no you won't. And that's really going to bum you out. But it'll be ok.*

Fast-forward past the ear chopping and the arrest, and we see Peter does abandon Jesus, and does deny knowing him three times. Ouch. This one hurts. I know I can relate to making huge promises to God. I know I have had the noblest intentions. I know I've spoken boldly, and then failed. Gotten scared. Bailed.

The Bible says that after Peter denied knowing Jesus, he went away, "Weeping bitterly." I don't know if you've ever seen a grown man weep bitterly, but it's not pretty. Peter let himself down, but so much worse, he let Jesus down. And I think that's when we all weep the bitterest tears.

I Know You

Then there's this one last time that I want to mention here. Jesus and the disciples are just kind of hanging out. (I imagine this is how they spent a lot of their time since Netflix wasn't a thing). Can you imagine just hanging out with Jesus? He was probably so bad at small talk. *What's new with you? Never mind, I know exactly what's new with you, and you need to cut some of it out.* So, as you would expect, Jesus brings up a kind of heavy subject. He asks the disciples what people are saying about him, which was kind of like Googling yourself back then.

"Guys, who do people say I am?"

"Well, you know Jesus, some people think you're John the Baptist, some people think you're Elijah, some are saying Jeremiah or one of the other prophets. Public opinion is pretty varied."

"Well, who do *you* think I am?"

Enter Peter.

"You are the Messiah. The son of the living God." (Some of my wording, but pretty close to the real thing).

Peter gets one right!

The guy is all over the place throughout most of the gospels, but in this instance, Peter hits the nail on the head. Peter gets the most important question correct, and Jesus is thrilled with this answer. So thrilled he changes Peter's name (to Peter from Simon). He goes on to tell Peter that he is going to build his church upon this rock. Upon him, which is quite the honor.

Peter made a lot of mistakes in his life. I've only mentioned a few, but Peter overreacting, saying something dumb, or making a rash decision is a pretty common theme throughout the gospels. But in this instance, he gets the question right when it matters. Jesus is the Messiah.

And that's the only one we need to get right as well. There are lots of questions surrounding Christianity and faith in general, and it's tempting to try to answer all of them at once. But we don't have to do that. Peter really only got the one right, and he got to be "The Rock." We can mix up, screw up, and mess up the rest of it. But if we have that one right, I wouldn't be too worried about the rest.

A lot of Christian folklore has St. Peter sitting outside of the pearly gates (By the way, why? Why use pearls on gates? Follow-up question; why does heaven need gates?), deciding who gets to enter heaven and who doesn't. I kind of hope that's true, because I assume he would only ask us one question.

And if nothing else, at least I never cut anyone's ear off.

Homeless: *Adjective*

This Time Was Different

Some time ago now, I was running some errands. It was a cold day, and it had snowed recently. I think it was a Thursday. That afternoon, I met a homeless man. He was standing on the side of the road, holding a sign that simply read "Homeless." So, as I stopped at a light near him, I checked if I had any cash. I did, so I rolled down my passenger side window, and waved to him.

This is usually a pretty rehearsed interaction for both of us. They walk over; I hand them some cash, they say something like "God bless, thank you," and I say something like "Good luck, you got this." But this interaction was different, even from the time I waved him over.

He seemed surprised by this, almost like he didn't know what to do. He made his way over, through the snow, to my car, and didn't say anything. He just leaned down and looked at me. He wasn't much older than me. He made eye contact, which was strange for me.

His eyes were full of pain, and they looked like they may have been welling up with tears. I really didn't know what to do with this, so I held eye contact, and reached out with the cash, that happened to be around five bucks; nothing significant. He quietly took it. No "God bless" no "Thank you;" he barely got any words out at all. He tried to.

"Thank you so much man… I just…" And his voice trailed off.

I don't remember what I said. Probably nothing. We both nodded our understanding, and he made his way back through the snow to his corner. He waved his thanks again as I drove by him. I've had this same interaction a dozen times. But this time, it was different.

It was worse.

To make it even worse, I was on my way to a grocery store. I was on my way to an enormous store with aisles and aisles of food and junk, all of it at my disposal. Not only do I have access to food, I have access to food that I *like*. Sometimes I buy food just because it sounds good to me. Sometimes, I throw food away because I forgot about it in my fridge and it turned green. I was on my way to a place that could feed hundreds of people. And he was still standing there.

This was the first time I ever saw a homeless person for what he was. A person. A person who did not have a home. I parked in the parking lot and sat for quite a while. Just thinking. I can still see the look on his face. It just screamed, *This isn't what was supposed to happen*. I didn't get his name. But I think about him often.

Some Of Us Would Like To Talk About Fishing At This Point

We could use this opportunity to talk about fishing if you want. We could talk about whether I fed him for a day or for life. A temporary solution instead of a long term one. But I don't want to. Mostly because I think feeding someone for a day is a good thing, but also because these conversations never seem to be productive. Honestly, I don't care if you start giving homeless people some change, or some cash, or a fish, or a fishing pole, or nothing.

None of this bothers me. My job isn't to know his story. My job isn't to monitor what he does with the money afterward. My job isn't to force him to make the decisions I want him to make. My job is to express my faith through love, as best I can, when I can. My job is to be Jesus' love. And I don't think love worries about all of these things. I think it just sees someone who has a need and meets it the best it can. Even if it's not much, it tries.

And I think the best way I can love him from my car at a red light is to give him a chance. Sometimes, people just need to be given a few fish to get them through until they learn how to fish.

But this chapter isn't actually about homeless people and if we should give them money or not. I'm going to keep using it as an example, but I'd rather talk about a word we need to rethink, a verse I needed to reread, and what Jesus has to say about all of this.

I Say Potato Nobody Says Pahtahto

The word I would like us to discuss is homeless. Homeless is a word we use to describe people without a home. (Brilliant,

Homeless: Adjective

I know). My concern is that we've stopped using the word homeless to describe *people*, and have started using it as a word in place of people. Let me show you what I mean.

We've gotten into the habit of taking the phrase "Homeless person" and substituting it with "Homeless," or "The homeless." What we've done here is taken an adjective and turned it into a noun. Now instead of seeing a homeless person, we see one of the homeless. We've taken what they are, a person, and turned it into something else.

Something less.

We need to remember when we see someone on the side of the road that they are a person without a home, not a member of the homeless. They are a thinking, feeling, living, breathing person the same as you and me; the same as our sons or daughters, the same as our friends, the same as our parents. Exactly the same.

Homeless is not a noun. It is an adjective used to describe individuals who are just as loved as us, and deserve everything we deserve.

This may seem like simple semantics, and to an extent, it is, but my goal here is not to correct our grammar. My goal is for us to reshape and correct the mentality that we approach people with because homelessness is only one example of where we do this in our lives. If we start to look for it, we can see it all around us.

We take a situation, and we allow it to define a person. The family struggling through a job loss, the girl with the reputation, the co-worker with the nickname, the neighbor with the kid that's always in trouble, the acquaintance with the addiction, or whoever it is for us. We take adjectives, and we turn them into nouns. We take people and turn them into less.

As Christ followers, we have to see these people. We have to see these *people*. We have to be able to see them for what they are, and not simply see their situation. We can't just drive by. We can't assume someone else will help. We have to *see* them.

What We All Want

When I see a homeless person I start with the assumption that they do not want to be homeless. This seems like an obvious point, but when was the last time we really thought about it? When we go by a homeless person, isn't there, at least, a small part of us that, in the back of our mind, says, *They're used to it. They don't mind. Their decisions landed them here*? We know intellectually that it's not true, and yet, I often forget that homeless people are exactly that: People.

Exactly the same as me. Exactly the same as you. Homeless people have dreams; they have hopes. They have desires and goals. They want families, they want a retirement plan, they want to watch *The Bachelor*, and cook hot dogs on a grill, and drive a motorcycle, and go to Disneyland. They want all of these things, and yet I find myself assuming that because they're homeless, they're somehow different.

We see people in situations they don't want to be in all the time, and for some reason our default setting is to assume they can do something about it. It's like we look at someone who needs help and think, *Why are they doing that?* It's like we forget that they don't want to be where they are either. We forget that their situation is helpless.

Now, while I do want us to start looking specifically at homeless people differently, this idea applies to many more. The idea of looking people in the eye, of understanding that they have the same dreams as us and that they are just as deserving of those dreams applies to all people. Looking at people as people rather than adjectives applies to all people.

Homeless individuals have a special place in my heart, but they may not in yours. That's okay; homelessness may not be *your one thing*. But helping people that can't help themselves has to be our thing. That part isn't optional.

Jesus And The Least Of These

Jesus uses the phrase "The least of these" to describe people who find themselves in a helpless situation. It refers to people who can't help themselves. He uses the specific examples of being Hungry, Thirsty, a Stranger, Naked, Sick and In Prison. These are all helpless situations. Nobody is doing any of them if they can do something about it for themselves.

He uses these examples to make a point. His point being that we need to care for people who find themselves in situations like these. He says that anything we do for these people, we do for him. When we serve someone, it's like we're serving Jesus. When we help someone who needs help, it's like we're helping Jesus.

This is where many of us stop.

Of course we should help people! It's just like we're helping Jesus!

While that's not a terrible takeaway and is something we should do (That's how I learned it in Sunday school) it's not the whole story.

Because then, Jesus says something really crazy. (And really terrifying). He goes on to say,

> "I tell you the truth, when you refused to help the least of these my brothers and sisters, you were refusing to help me."

Honestly, I'm pretty comfortable with the first part. Every time I do something nice, I do it for Jesus. That sounds great. But every time I *don't* do something nice?

Yikes.

It's the same as not helping Jesus. None of us would leave Jesus in a helpless situation. We would never even think about it. And yet, Jesus is saying every time we walk by the least of these and avoid eye contact; we're avoiding eye contact with Jesus. Every time we don't feel like it, think someone else will do it, or don't think it's our problem, we're not helping Jesus. Every time we reduce someone to their situation, it's like we reduce Jesus.

In Summary

We're all going to encounter the least of these in our lives in different ways. Some of us interact with homeless people regularly. Some of us never do. But we all encounter the least of these. We all encounter people that can't help themselves. We all encounter people in helpless situations.

Some of us know someone that lost a job. Some of us have a friend that's getting bullied. Many of us know a social outcast. We know a lonely person. Someone who's grown bitter. We know someone living paycheck to paycheck.

We know we have the resources, we know we could make the time, we even know that doing something wouldn't be that hard. The truth is, for some of us, we just don't feel like it. Maybe that's part of why we feel so much guilt when we think about the least of these. We know we could do something. We know we would never leave Jesus in that situation.

We would never reduce Jesus to an adjective.

So, in summary.

The least of these are the people in our lives who find themselves in helpless situations.

We all have these people in our lives.

When we encounter these people, we need to see them as people. Not as their situations.

When we look at these people, we are seeing Jesus, whether we help them or not.

So we should help them.

I think if I was going to sum this chapter up in one phrase, it would be: *see people as people*. No matter what they're going through, the decisions they've made, or what they're doing. They deserve everything we deserve because they're people too. Because they're Jesus too.

We Can Do Better Than This. Part 2

You ready for another chapter of this nonsense?

Guys, we can do better. So much better. In so many ways. We're just getting started.

Round Two!

Price Check On Aisle 1930s

Okay, so you're in a grocery store. And you're thinking; *I don't know how to scan this cantaloupe, what a barcode is, how money works, or what store I'm in… I think I'll use the self-checkout…*

Guys, we're better than this.

This isn't the time to try something new. We can't be waiting for rush hour at grocery stores to try the self-checkout by ourselves for the first time. Look, I'm not the only one who believes there should be a brief application process to use the self-checkout line. I got in this line because it's supposed to be faster. Please stop trying to scan that individual grape.

Someone can help you over there Eleanor.

Feel free to pay by check.

Long Shorts, Or Short Longs

Okay, so you're a man. And you're thinking; *My shorts only approach mid-thigh length. This is fine.*

Umm…No?

You're better than that man. You're a man; your legs are gross. It's just the way it is. Nobody wants to see your curly black leg hairs coming at them. I mean, you do you, wear what you like.

Just don't sit next to me.

And wear longer shorts.

(Of course, there are exceptions to every rule. But in this case, they involve very specific events in which one is particularly skilled, like running great distances or swimming competitively. The neighborhood barbeque is not the place to break out the short jorts. There is a time and place for jorts. The time was 1980).

Surprise Nudity

Okay, so you had a baby. And you think, *I think I'll send a picture of my baby's naked butt to my friend.*

Why?

How this became a thing, I will never understand. Why the naked baby pictures? It's not like we could ever have a conversation like:

> Do you want to see a picture of my baby?
>
> Sure.
>
> Do you want to see a picture of my baby's butt?
>
> Of course not.
>
> Well, I already sent it to you in the form of a magnet. And I'm coming to visit in six months, and I expect it to be displayed on your fridge.

Yeah, it's a cute baby. Yes, I'm excited for you. No, I don't want to see your baby's butt. It's weird. Put some of those stretchy jeans for babies on it. You (And your baby) can do better than this.

Red Hoodie Guy

So, you're in a restaurant, and you decide to start watching a video on your phone. Loudly. C'mon. We're better than this. Seriously, what makes you think I want to hear this? Why do you feel that this is okay? If someone is having a loud conversation behind you, it's annoying. And yet, if you want to watch someone else have a conversation on your phone loudly, we feel this is fine? It's not.

(I'm looking at you red hoodie guy that's doing this as I'm writing this in Panera. I won't say your name here, because I don't know it. Maybe you should use that phone to order some headphones for yourself. And a new sweatshirt. That one is looking grungy).

It Can't Get Worse Than This Conversation

Okay, so I'm talking to someone about my baby. And I mention something that is frustrating in the moment. Maybe that I have to change a lot of diapers, maybe that I have to stay up at night, or bath time, or who knows what. And they have older children, so they decide to grace me with this sage advice,

Oh…just wait. It only gets worse.

We can do so much better than this. In what universe is it helpful for me to understand that things are going to get worse? What am I supposed to do with this information? *Heavens! I better get moving quickly before things get worse!*

If it's important to you that I know that you are suffering more than me right now, fine. We can talk about you. I can only assume that when your children need help with their homework, you have the same advice.

Oh… just wait until you get to high school. Homework will take longer then.

In which case, just wait until your kids are teenagers. It's going to get a lot worse.

Bless You?

Okay, so someone sneezes. What do we do? If you're like me, you don't do anything. Because sneezing is as natural and normal as blinking. But occasionally, someone will look at me after they sneeze. Like I'm supposed to now participate in some way.

And I know what they want. *Oh, I know what they want.* They want a blessing.

Much like Jacob, they will wrestle me with their stare until they get the blessing they desire. But we don't give the blessing. Because it's a silly thing to do, and we can do better than silly.

First, my blessing is worthless. You gain nothing from it. Blessing people is not something I've been trained to do.

Plus, I don't think it's fair. I'm not someone who sneezes very often. Do I not deserve to be blessed? *Blessed are those who sneeze, theirs is the blessing of those who conform to strange antiquated social norms.* My wife sneezes like 500 times a day. She'd be the ding dang pope if I blessed her every time. So I'm not doing it.

From here on, I think I'll say, *You just sneezed* when someone's waiting for my blessing. This is the maximum amount of participation I'm willing to have in someone else's sneeze.

Catch Up

So, you know when you squirt ketchup out of a bottle, and then there's that little bit of residual ketchup that just kind of makes its way onto the lid of the bottle…and then some monster just slams the lid right back on saving this red wedding disaster for the next person? Why? And more importantly; how? How does one go to sleep at night knowing these disgusting things they've done?

We can do better than this guys. I was just hoping that someone would dry out some ketchup or mustard on the rim of the bottle for me to drop onto my burger and not be able to find. I'll just look forward to this texture sensation of condiment concentrate mid-bite.

Gag.

Just a quick swipe of the napkin is all it takes to avoid this ketchup catastrophe. Give a squirt.

Decorative Bicycle

So, you have something. And you don't really want it. Perhaps it doesn't work. Or it's just an old something. So, one decides instead of throwing it in the trash it is going to become a decoration.

(This one bothers me in particular because when we moved into our home, there were like 30 baskets hanging from the ceiling of our basement. It was honestly terrifying. Why hang baskets from the ceiling? It really looked like the behavior of a crazy person. Anyway).

Guys, we can do better than this.

We know you don't use that typewriter on your desk.

We don't know why you have a painted bicycle in the corner.

That clock is broken. Hanging it upside down does not make it ironic or post-modern.

We don't need to put weird things on display. Just throw them away and hang a picture of dogs playing cards.

Since I have ALL Of Your Attention

Can we talk about group texts for a moment? Can we talk about group text courtesy for a brief moment? Can we talk about a group of people all answering the same question fifteen times in a row, resulting in your phone vibrating off the table? Guys, we can do better than this.

This isn't hard. One person has a question for fifteen people. They want 15 responses. The rest of us do not. I now know the entire guest list of a party that I have absolutely no interest in!

Wait… my wife just said she's looking forward to it. Hold on, let me respond quick.

*I'll be there too guys! *tongue out emoji* Looking forward to it!*

Anyway. Group texts are the worst.

#FoodPic

Look. I get the pictures of food, sometimes. You went to a nice restaurant, you got a fancy drink, it's something you've never seen before, will never see again, and you want to remember it. This is fine.

I do not understand the picture of the grilled cheese you made yourself.

We Can Do Better Than This. Part 2

We can do better than this guys. We get it; you're eating. But do we really need to be documenting oatmeal? Is this one of those moments you want forever?

And for the love of Christmas, please don't ask me to wait to start eating so you can document your calories. Feel free to snap a picture of me eating while your fries get cold. #MyIdiotHusbandTookABiteBeforeICouldGetAPicOfThis

Keep Baby Asleep

One Sleepless Night

At every point in any parent's life, they realize their priorities have shifted, and everything else is now secondary to this one all-important priority:

Keep. Baby. Asleep.

Nothing else really matters. Suddenly, you hear yourself saying things like,

"We can't watch that movie right now; it could wake the baby."

"You can't run the microwave right now; it might wake the baby."

"I can't go to the bathroom right now, because it will wake up the baby, and I'd rather just deal with *this*, than a crying baby right now."

I realized just how far this priority had seeped into my mind one fateful night when my daughter was around five months old.

Now, before I tell you this story, there are two things you should know. One, not everyone knows this, so I will tell you; baby finger-nails are like little tiny razor blades. They are sharp, and it really doesn't matter how often you trim them, they will cut you like you're made of tissue paper.

Two, I sleep without a shirt on, and on this fateful night, I didn't put one on. (Don't get ahead of me).

One night, our daughter woke up. And as babies do when they wake up, she started yelling at us about it. It was my turn, so I got up to rock her back to sleep. I picked her up, and all was going well, she was starting to settle down, and I'm thinking *this is going to be an easy one.*

As she is starting to settle down, I realize there is a reason for this. Her little hand has made its way up to my chest and has grabbed on to a strategic hand-hold that she's found. It's exactly where you think. Dead center, off to the left, a slightly raised portion of the chest…I'm not going to say where she grabbed on. But it rhymes with "ripple." For some reason, she has grabbed on, and this is calming to her.

With all of her five-month-old, razor talon, surprisingly powerful, grip strength, she grabs on. She grabs with all of her might and refuses to let go for any reason. For some reason, she has decided that this makes her happy. Even if it makes me so, very, very, unhappy. (Keeping in mind that one minute ago, I was asleep. And I've now woken to have a mousetrap of death clamped on to my chest). And I had a decision to make.

Everything in my entire body is screaming, "GETITOFF GETITOFF GETITOFF!!!" And yet, an even louder voice is saying in the back of my mind;

Keep. Baby. Asleep.

So, I did it. I just waited until her little hand loosened its death grip signaling that she had drifted back to a peaceful sleep. I set her down, got myself an ice pack, and went back to sleep. (By the way, my wife is watching all of this and is silently dying of laughter, while I'm silently dying of discomfort).

What's so interesting about this story to me is how my priorities shifted. Without me doing anything, suddenly my desire to sleep through the night was more important to me than my desire to not be in significant physical discomfort. This is interesting because I never sat down and chose this priority. I never decided that this was going to be important to me. It just kind of happened.

Slippery Slope

That's the funny thing about our priorities. They will just shift and change on us, without our permission. As time goes and our lives change, our priorities just kind of shift around. We don't plan it, we don't fill out a form, but suddenly, what was very important to us no longer matters. And perhaps even more surprising is that things we didn't even know existed are now our top priorities.

It's funny how the world has a way of making odd things priorities for us, isn't it? Children cannot imagine prioritizing the sleep of an infant over avoiding aggressive chest torment. They also can't imagine prioritizing a job over a family, or weight loss over a cheeseburger, or cigarettes over health, or golf over a child's soccer game, or alcohol over a relationship, or many of the things that just, sort of, became important to us. We didn't plan to have these things be the most important in our lives; it just kind of happens.

The thing about priorities is they will *just kind of happen* unless we choose them.

And there, my friends, is the good news. We can choose! And we need to choose very carefully because there is a lot to choose from. Jobs, family time, fitness, crocheting, golf, television, cooking, cleaning, yardwork, kid's events, fishing, hiking, badminton, bike riding, house projects, writing, career advancement, school, karate…we have 24 hours each day. We're just not going to get to all of it. We have to pick carefully.

Isn't it interesting that faith is often the first one to *just kind of* stop? It's so easy to just start sleeping in on Sunday mornings. It's so easy to just start working a little earlier instead of praying. It's so easy to just let grandma take the kids to church. It's easy to put Jesus on the shelf for a while.

Isn't that funny? Isn't it so weird that the one thing that should be a no-brainer as a priority is often the *very first* to get cut? Isn't it odd that the most important part of our life is often the part we have a hard time making a priority?

When My Priorities Shifted

I remember being a youth pastor. A YOUTH PASTOR! Like, at a church, and realizing the only time I prayed was in front of people. The only time I read my bible was when I was preparing a lesson. I never worshiped because Sunday mornings had become work. I was distracted, and I didn't have my own time. My focus time in the mornings had become *me time*. It just kind of happened.

Much like my priorities had shifted toward "Keep. Baby. Asleep," my priorities shifted away from Jesus and toward me.

I tell you this just to show you that, it happens! It happens to all of us. Life happens, things happen; we get distracted, we get tunnel vision, and our priorities change. That's okay, as long as we're reassessing from time to time. Is our faith still a top priority? Is our family still a top priority? Is our health still a top priority? Are your priorities *your* priorities? Or were they chosen for you?

My daughter sleeps just fine while I'm writing this, and it's much less important to me to "keep baby asleep." New priorities have taken its place, and new ones will replace these. As long as we understand that our focus will change over time, and we continually refocus, we'll do just fine. So, it makes sense that we need to have a time each day where we re-focus.

A *focus time* if you will.

Focus Up

When I'm explaining the concept of a quiet time to teenage guys, I use the term Focus Time. I use this term because it describes exactly what it is. It's a time we take out of our day to focus on our goal.

I like to think of an athlete sitting in the locker room before the big game starts. There are plenty of distractions. The sound of the crowd roaring overhead, other players fidgeting about nervously in the locker room, things that happened before the game, responsibilities afterward. But right now, our athlete sits calmly, silently meditating on the task at hand. Spending a few minutes being laser-focused on their goal. That's the mentality I like to approach my focus time with. A short time set aside to do nothing but focus on our goal.

Maybe the idea of a "quiet time" sounds boring, or even overwhelming.

> *Where would I start?*
> *The Bible is a big place.*
> *Which version should I use?*
> *I always get distracted when I pray.*
> *Should I use a study guide/book?*
> *Whose guide/book is trustworthy?*
> *I always fall asleep when I read the Bible.*

You don't have to know any of that. You just have to take your first step based on what you do know. And we know now, that our priorities will naturally shift away from our goals unless we consciously keep them focused. So, we need to focus regularly. *But I'm still not sure where to start. Nothing I've tried in the past has worked.* Fine. We'll start small. Let's look at a few examples.

The Bible Tells Me Something

Maybe you decide that you do want to incorporate a Bible reading time into your focus time each day. That's great, but you've tried this before, and you hit some parts that were weird, then some parts that were redundant, and then some that were so terribly dry (both because they were boring and were set in the desert), and then parts that were just long lists of rules that really didn't seem applicable today, and you quit. Yeah, the beginning of the Bible is hard. (There. I said it). It requires a little more understanding and study to really enjoy. Luckily, you don't have to start there.

Start with a quick Google search, and search for something you want to know more about. Maybe it's Jesus, maybe it's some of the stories you've heard, maybe there's a verse you've heard before and want to read the part it's in. Look, it's perfectly fine to search,

"Parts of the Bible that are easy to understand."

"Parts of the Bible that talk about courage."

"Where is Jesus found in the Bible?" (I'm sure it's not your most embarrassing Google search)

This is a perfectly acceptable place to start. If you want my personal recommendation, I'd say check out one of the gospels: Mathew, Mark, Luke, or John. (Which is where Jesus is found in the Bible). And I'd suggest starting with John. Start there. There will be time for lengthy studies in Deuteronomy someday. For now, just get started.

Dear Jesus... Are We Out Of Milk?

Maybe you've also decided that you want prayer to be part of your daily focus time. Great! But, you have a hard time praying. You've noticed that anytime you start praying, your mind just kind of wanders, and suddenly, you're planning a vacation that you can't even afford. *How did I start thinking about my tan-lines in the first place...?* Or maybe you just have no idea what to pray about. Maybe you feel guilty about something and just don't feel right praying. These are all pretty common struggles with prayer. But, again, nobody is asking you to pray for an hour every morning and evening.

Maybe you set a goal that you are going to pray for five minutes a day. Honestly, that's a pretty long stretch when you're just getting started, so maybe you decide to break that up into five one minute prayers throughout your day. Maybe you even set an alarm that goes off every few hours to remind you to pray. That's great! (By the way, five minutes every day comes out to 35 minutes per week, about 2.3 hours per month, and around 29 hours per year. That's over a whole day of praying. Lives have been changed by less).

Prayer is very much about quality over quantity. We don't measure other relationships by how long we talk, but by the quality of the conversations we have. And with any relationship, as the conversations get better and easier, they tend to get longer.

You Mean The Internet Isn't Evil?

But maybe reading and praying just aren't your thing yet. It's possible the idea of reading any book, let alone a notoriously complicated book, is just too daunting for you. Okay, maybe YouTube is more your style right now. There are seriously so many great resources available for free on the internet, and YouTube is a great place to get started. Maybe you want to watch half of a sermon every morning, or a devotional video series might be a better fit for you. You can spend some time searching for your favorite Christian YouTube channels until you find a great fit that helps you focus.

Once again, start by just searching for what you want. Maybe you search for

"Sermon about peace."

"Videos on tithing."

"Is cursing sinful?"

"Videos to quit porn."

"Sermon on gratitude."

These are all fine places to start.

You can find anything you're looking for, and this is a great way to get started with resetting your focus if you don't want to get started with reading just yet.

There are so many resources from books, to podcasts, to videos, to live conferences to all of the Christian music available to help you refocus and keep Jesus a priority in your life. Don't feel locked into the classic quiet time/devotional/devos/prayer time model so many of us have heard. Reconnect with God and do it your way. Get started. Start with what feels easy, and work toward doing more. Trust me; you'll want more once you get started.

ReFocus

And before you say it, I know you're thinking: you would if you *could just find the time*. Don't use this excuse. You have the time; you're just not making it a priority. Whatever we make a priority gets the time. It doesn't have to take long, some days will be shorter than others, but you need to just make the time. (By the way, right now, you're reading a book…so, I know you have at least a little free time). It's important. It's a major way we keep Jesus a priority in our life. Make the time.

Guys, believe me, God is not going to be disappointed because you don't meditate for half an hour, read two books of the Bible, and pray for everyone you know every day. He's just going to be so pumped about the time you are spending together, even if it's just the easy part for now. And by the way, I think you're really going to enjoy it too.

I'm sure you'll find that you want more eventually, but for now, start small, don't get overwhelmed, and don't worry if you miss a day here and there. If you don't want your priorities to be set for you, focus up, and set them yourself. If we're going to express our faith through love, Jesus has to be a top priority for us.

Guys, it is imperative that Jesus doesn't become something that just kind of stops being important. Jesus cannot be something that we used to really be into, but not so much anymore. Jesus cannot fade away in our lives. The world will naturally try to make other things more important. Our priorities will just kind of move and shift if we're not careful. We have to re-focus-every day. So, focus up.

And most importantly, always put a shirt on when picking up a baby.

Handing Out Love From A Cardboard Box

It's A Bird, It's A Plane, No! It's Creepy Comb-over Guy!

I mentioned that I went back to school a few years ago, which gave me the strange opportunity to spend time on a college campus as an adult, with all the perks that come with spending time on a college campus, including paying for parking, listening to college students whine about things I don't understand, and feeling really old. One day, as I was walking across a particularly crowded parking lot, I noticed a man standing on the sidewalk by the entrance to my building. I made a note of his appearance.

He was a little disheveled looking with green pants and a blue windbreaker over his neutral colored polo. He was older than me, probably in his mid-fifties. He had large glasses with the lenses that turn into sunglasses when you go outside and an elaborate comb-over. He didn't really smile and had kind of a creepy vibe to him. At least it was daylight.

As I approached, I realized he was talking to other students as they entered the building, and was trying to hand something out to them. When it was my turn, he looked at me and said,

"How about a free New Testament from *such and such* church?"

I then noticed that he had a cardboard box next to him full of New Testaments that he was attempting to hand out to college students. I politely declined and explained to him that I had the Bible on an app on my phone already, and didn't need another copy. He nodded, and I went to class.

Initially, I was annoyed.

Really guy? This is the best you can do?

You sat down and thought, *I should go tell people about Jesus, what's the best way to do that? I guess I'll wear something weird and try to hand out a notoriously complicated and misunderstood book to people half my age on a Tuesday.*

I was annoyed half way really. On one hand, *he's trying.* He's doing something, which is more than we can say for many people. At least he's doing something. But on the other hand… this is a terrible plan!

I think what bothered me was just how little thought and effort must have gone into this plan, and that the same Jesus I represent, is now being represented by creepy cardboard guy. It just felt like the greatest news a person can hear in their life deserved a little better execution than this. It just didn't feel like this was the best way to introduce someone to Jesus.

People Will Notice... Will They?

It feels like we put such a heavy emphasis on telling people about Jesus, and I really don't think we need to. (Stay with me). I've mentioned before that I was taught that you need to be ready to have a conversation with someone at any given moment about Jesus. You need to be able to defend everything you believe, and that "saving lost souls" was the most important thing you can do in your life. I was taught different techniques about how to strike up these conversations, and basically how to force Jesus into someone's life.

Now, I think having conversations are important, but I don't think they need to be forced. I think inviting someone to church is a great thing to do, but it probably shouldn't be the first thing we say to someone. I do think it is important for us to introduce people to Jesus. I just think there's a better way.

Check out this story about Jesus.

Jesus is sitting with his disciples eating dinner the night he is going to be killed. So, this is one of the last times he's going to be able to talk to them. It's interesting to me what he says to them. He doesn't tell them to tell everyone about what they are about to see. He doesn't emphasize walking up to strangers or reaching the lost, or making converts. He tells them to love each other. He says that's how the world will recognize them.

People will know us by our love. That's the new commandment Jesus gives.

I always thought that was such a stupid answer when I was growing up. *People will notice there is something different about you and want to know about it...* That never made sense to me. But the truth is, love stands out. It probably won't result in a conversation in which you need to defend your faith, as I was led to believe, but it will never go unnoticed.

And getting noticed can be hard these days. Companies and marketing firms spend millions (literally) of dollars trying to figure out ways to get our attention. Market research, commercials, focus groups, billboards, advertisements, all exist just to get our attention. As it turns out, Jesus knew more about marketing than anyone.

I probably spend too much time on social media (we all do), but I think there is a simple demonstration of this to be found in how we interact online. Right now, the political climate is a mess. The social issues platform is a mess. Non-political issues are a mess. Conversations are not civil, and people are mad. People are angry about guns, and abortion, and immigration, and LGBT rights, and pipelines…people are angry. And when people are angry they share short videos about what they are angry about.

But you know what videos keep going viral? The really happy ones. They have way more views than the angry ones.

The videos of people finding new ways to help each other have more views than the one about the political candidate being stupid. The video of the pro bono work being done by doctors has way more views than the angry guy and his theory on gun control. The one where teachers are going above and beyond for their students show up far more often than the mom-shaming lady.

The happy ones stand out. The loving ones stand out.

Isn't that strange? People will have arguments about anything, fight with strangers, share angry memes, and tweet nasty comments. But at the end of the day, we like to watch videos of people doing the right thing. We like to see evidence of progress. We love to see love at work.

Love stands out.

Love moves people. Love attracts people. Heck, love confuses people. It draws us in. It inspires us. We want to be a part of it when we see it. We want there to be more of it when we see it. Love is powerful. It's the most powerful force in the world.

Andy, didn't you already cover this in this book? Yeah, kind of. But maybe, just maybe it needs to be re-emphasized. There's a lot of misinformation floating around about what expressing our faith looks like, and I just feel like we can do better than creepy or scary. This message deserves that.

Love is more powerful than hermeneutics, or apologetics (Fancy words for studying the Bible and defending your faith). It's more powerful than any conversation or point you can have. I'm not going to try to say it better than Bob Goff. He wrote in his book *Love Does,*

> "If you want to share your faith, go love someone. You just did."

We are going to be known for the love we show people, not the arguments we win. We will be known for the people we serve, not the airtight exegesis we perform. We'll be known for who we are helping, not the number of church attendees we have. We'll be known for who we love.

Why Are We Trying Anything Else?

Love is our most powerful weapon. Why are we trying to use others?

This is our best option for introducing people to Jesus. Why we so often opt for the second or third option makes no sense to me. If we really want people to meet Jesus, wouldn't we be doing the very best that we can? Wouldn't we start with our best option? Why don't we start with the best part?

Companies that are selling hamburgers are working day and night to get a product into our hands. They dedicate time, effort, and money to telling us about their products. And the best we can do is try to have a conversation with our co-workers is if comes up naturally? The best we can do is hand out books from a cardboard box? We have the best news in the world, and we put no effort into telling people about it!?

Why are we not using our most powerful weapon? Why are we resorting to minimal effort attempts? Why are we trying to force conversation when we all know actions speak louder than words? (Some things become a cliché for a reason). Why are we teaching students and adults to defend their faith, to know all the answers, when we should be helping them love the people they want to save?

We are not going to be able to cut through the noise of everything else. There are too many negative voices out there for us to try to shout over. Why do we think people want to hear another voice shouting anyway? We're sick of people shouting at us. Radical love will cut through the noise. People will notice radical love.

The good news here is you don't need to feel obligated to have painful conversations with your co-workers anymore. You don't have to feel guilty that you haven't tried to evangelize to your neighbors.

The bad news is we have to do something harder. We have to try to be Jesus to people.

A lot of times, we don't want to introduce people to Jesus because we think it will be awkward. But love is never awkward! Sometimes, it looks a little weird, and sometimes, it takes us out of our comfort zone. But never awkward. People understand love.

I guess what I'm getting at here is, if we want to introduce people to Jesus, and that's really our goal, we should try to find the absolute best way to do it. I have a hard time believing Christians are sitting down and thinking the best way to introduce people to Jesus is through direct mailers, street preaching, handing out New Testaments, or striking up awkward conversations with strangers. I don't remember Jesus using awkward forced strategies to talk to people. They just wanted to be near him. They were just drawn to that kind of love.

And I think that's how it should be for us. I really don't like some of the stereotypes that surround Christianity. You know what they are. And it's a shame because the one thing we should be known for is how we love each other.

It's hard to hand love out of a cardboard box, but people will notice.

People always notice love.

The Last Chapter

We made it! We've covered quite a bit of ground here haven't we? Thanks for sticking with me and reading this whole book; it honestly means a lot to me.

I'm never quite sure how to end anything. Blog posts, videos, conversations…it always feels so abrupt. But really, what else is there to say? We've covered:

How to handle clowns,

What is and is not appropriate for a barbeque,

How to get in great shape if you're in third grade,

Greeting time,

Baby butt pictures,

Burritos (Wait, did we talk about burritos? Oh well, next time.)

Liam Neeson,

Bumper Stickers,

Comb-overs,

What to do if you're trapped in a van with gaseous teenagers,

Substitute teaching,

And a lot more.

I hope it was fun to read. I enjoyed writing it.

But more than that, I hope you decided to take action because of something in this book. I hope it inspired you, or annoyed you, or made you think about something enough to do something about it.

I hope it made you want to express your faith through love.

I know we've talked about it a lot. (I know. If I mention it one more time you're going to scream.) And we've talked about in a lot of different ways. I don't want you to try to put everything we've talked about into action. I would love it if you did, but you don't need to put everything from every chapter into practice. (That sounds exhausting). My guess is one thing stood out to you from this book. There was probably one section where you thought, *You know, this guy may actually have a point there.*

Do that.

Actually do it. Don't just underline it and never re-read it. Do it. Put it into practice. Be bad at it for a while. Practice. Whatever it is. Get started.

This world needs more Jesus.

What is your one thing that you're going to start chasing after?

What is the easy part that you can do today?

Where are the least of these in your life that need you?

How are you going to push your own faith to Olympic levels?

How are you going to share Jesus' love in the least creepy and scary way possible?

What are you not going to be afraid of anymore?

How are you going to go from faith to faithful?

I Wanted To Come Up With Something Really Clever For The Last Subtitle, But Couldn't

I had the privilege of working at a Christian summer camp for students one summer. We would have them for five days, during which we tried our very best to inspire and challenge them as best we could. It was incredible. We had so many amazing conversations with students, and we heard even more stories about life change. I always wanted to make sure students were intentional about what changes they were going to make after camp. So, on the last night I would always ask them the same question.

What's going to be different when you go home?

What's going to be different? Specifically. They were inspired all week at camp; it would be a shame to go home and change nothing.

So, I'm going to ask you the same question. What's going to be different when you put this book down? It probably took you around five hours to read. You invested a few dollars to read it, you put in the time, you saw all of the words in it. What's going to be different? It would be a shame to read a book and not have a takeaway of any kind.

I'm going to leave a few lines at the bottom of this page for you to write what will be different. If you're like me, you won't do this. You'll just make a mental note and move on. But humor me. Write it down. What is going to be different now that you read this book? (If you're going to loan this book to a friend, you can write something cryptic or encoded). But put pen to paper.

Write it down.

Get started.

Start small.

Thanks again so much for reading it.

It's time to go from Faith to Faithful.

_____

_____

_____

Notes

Business School Theology

I should say thank you to Bob Goff and Andy Stanley for introducing me to this verse. It's one I've probably read a hundred times, but never really took note of before.

Nobody Likes Swimming

Mathew 16:24 -This is where Jesus says these crazy things

Galatians 2:20 -Paul talking about his old life being dead

A Clown In The Rain

Mathew 14 –The story about Jesus walking on water is in Mathew 14. Read the whole chapter. It really adds to the story.

Pete

Matthew 14 –Walking on water again

Mathew 16:23 –"Get behind me satan!"

John 18 –Jesus knocking people over and Peter cutting off someone's ear

Luke 22:15 –Jesus heals the ear

Luke 22:56-60 –Peter denying knowing Jesus

Luke 22:62 –Peter weeping bitterly

Matthew 16:13-19 –Peter gets one right

Holy

Check out John Crist on his website www.johncristcomedy.com or on Youtube www.youtube.com/user/johnbcrist. I'm sure you've already heard of him. If you've heard of me, you've heard of him. Anyway, check his stuff out. And check your heart.

Footprints poem –No idea how to reference this. My research indicates that we don't know who wrote it. Feel free to Google "Footprints poem" if you've somehow not heard it by now.

Isaiah 6:1-5 –Isaiah's vision

Shout out to Francis Chan for using this passage in a sermon, which really got me thinking about God's holiness in the first place.

Laundry, Nail-Care, Chinese food

I have no idea how to cite a comedian. I mentioned Bill Engvall in this chapter. Check him out at his website WWW.BillEngvall.com

The Easy Part

I John 3:17-18

Matthew 22:36-40 –Jesus' greatest commandment

Stupid People

Brown, Brené. Braving the Wilderness: The Quest for True Belonging and the Courage to Stand Alone. Farmington Hills, Mich: Thorndike Press, a Part of Gale, a Cengage Company, 2018

(Go read everything you can by Brene. I'd start with "I thought it was just me" but you really can't go wrong).

Your One Thing

Besson, Luc, and Robert Mark Kamen. *Taken*. 20th Century Fox Home Entertainment, 2008

(Such a good movie)

Homeless: *Adj*

Matthew 25:31-45 –The least of these

Handing Out Love From A Cardboard Box

Goff, Bob. Love Does. Nashville, TN: Thomas Nelson, 2014.

(Seriously go read Bob's books. I'm glad you read mine first, you won't like it after his).

John 13:34-35 –Jesus' new commandment

Thank You So Much To:

Wife. Let's start with an easy one. For your undying patience, support, and encouragement. Seriously I would never do any of this without you. Do you want to get some coffee this week?

Colbie. Little girl, little girl…what would I do without you? I'd write much faster for one. Thanks for distracting me, watching me write, and inspiring me. There's a whole chapter about you in this book. I can't wait to see what you do next.

David, Kary, the IS Tribe, and the AAE staff. For showing me how to create well, tell my story, and giving me this opportunity. Keep igniting souls.

Elizabeth at FreelancePlus. Thanks for catching my mistakes and making me sound smart. (Check her out on Fiverr.com for your editing needs!)

Zeljka Kojic for creating the stunning cover of this book. (Check her out at 99designs.com)

My friends at Blacklevel photography for the author pic. I think I look great.

Panera Bread for having unlimited free refills on coffee. Can you have some decaf ready for me tomorrow?

Anyone that let me bounce ideas off of them. There are too many of you to remember and mention here. You know who you are. You had more to do with this than you realize.

Cousin dinner. For asking how the book is going, during the precious little time we had before someone started crying.

LCBC, for helping me fill up every week, and inspiring me with new ideas.

Life group, for the laughs, the food and the conversation.

Anyone who appeared in any of the stories I told. I hope I did it justice.

Finally you. You who takes the time to read the thank you part of books. Thanks for reading this, I hope you enjoyed it.

Free Video Series on YouTube!

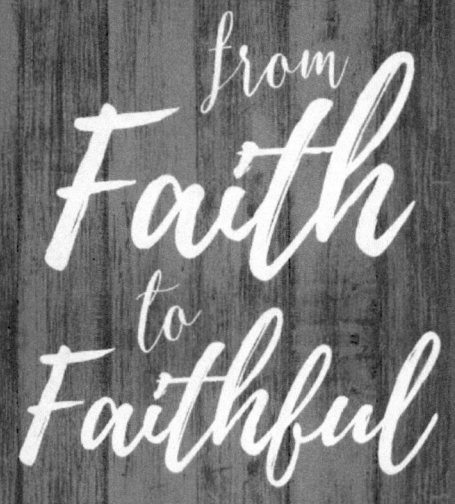

Watch the *From Faith to Faithful* video series free on YouTube. Perfect for your group or Bible study!

www.YouTube.com/C/AndyBuckwalter

Accompanying discussion questions available for free at AndyBuckwalter.com

BRING ANDY TO YOUR NEXT EVENT

Andy's humor and energy coupled with thought provoking content makes him the ideal speaker for your next event.

CONTACT ANDY TO START THE CONVERSATION

ANDYBUCKWALTER.COM

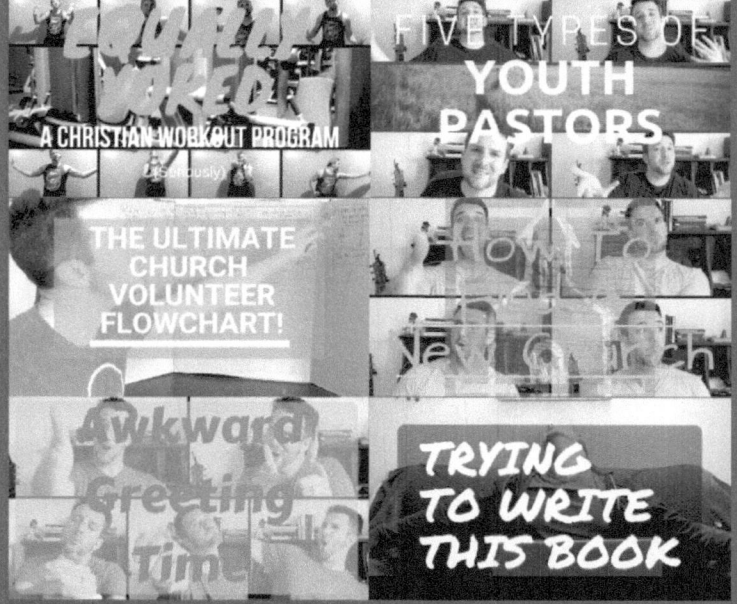

About The Author

Andy Buckwalter is husband to Leann and father to Colbie Joy and their growing family. He is also a writer, speaker, and video creator who challenges and inspires individuals to grow and deepen their walk with Jesus, so they can better express their faith through love to the world.

Connect at AndyBuckwalter.com

Email: Andy@AndyBuckwalter.com

Connect on Social media:

    Youtube: https://Youtube.com/c/AndyBuckwalter

    Twitter: https://twitter.com/AndyBuckwalter

    Instagram: https://www.instagram.com/Andy.Buckwalter

    Facebook: https://www.facebook.com/AndyBuckwalterAuthor/

www.ingramcontent.com/pod-product-compliance
Lightning Source LLC
LaVergne TN
LVHW041635060526
838200LV00040B/1583